Nobody Wants Your Child

Nobody Wants Your Child

Milton L. Creagh

Rock Hill Books of Georgia
Atlanta

Copyright © 2006 by Milton L. Creagh.

Nobody Wants Your Child
ISBN: 0-9776036-0-1
10 9 8 7 6 5 4 3 2 1

All Rights Reserved. Published in the United States by Rock Hill Books of Georgia, LLC. Some of the names of individuals mentioned in this book have been changed. No part of this publication may be reproduced without the prior written permission of the publisher.

Cover photographs by Amanda Rohde, Henry Beeker, and Tatiana Sayig.

Printed in the United States of America.

*To Mom and Dad. Thanks for raising kids
who found a world that indeed wanted them.*

Praise for Milton Creagh's Work

"*Parenting Works* is must viewing for parents who want to improve their skills."
—Dr. Alvin Poussaint

"*Parenting Works* is important, helpful television for families."
— Fred Rogers, *Mister Rogers' Neighborhood*

"[*Parenting Works* is] an innovative national public television series."
—*San Jose Mercury News*

"*Masquerade* host Milton Creagh blows the cover off of the many popular myths surrounding the hidden war with drug and alcohol addiction." —*Atlanta Inquirer*

"I have heard [Milton] speak on two other occasions, and he is the most powerful speaker I've ever heard."
—Dr. Henry Stewart
Dean of Library Services
Troy University

~~~ Contents ~~~

What in the World is Going On?

Have you ever had the feeling that you had just about seen it all and as a result nothing could shock, surprise or amaze you? Well, I used to feel that way until very recently. I am a consultant and speaker with over twenty years of experience, yet a couple of months ago I had two conversations that opened my eyes. (Or maybe I should say it in the vernacular I grew up with: *blew my mind.*) One conversation was with a senior vice president of a corporation that has been on my client list for a number of years. The second was with a mid-level manager of a new client. Until then I considered myself pretty shock proof. No more.

The mid-level manager I was lunching with shared with me that his organization had recently terminated a couple of young employees. Both were in their mid twenties. I became very curious when I heard that neither of them was considered a poor, problem or low performer.

The two terminated employees worked together in the same location and happened to be African-American males. (Get ready, this is where the shock part begins.) These two young men were counseled, warned and eventually fired for using the "N" word at work. For those of you a little out of touch, "N" word is the politically correct way to refer to the word *nigger.* In the *DK Illustrated Oxford Dictionary, nigger* is defined as: *a contemptuous term used for a black or dark-skinned person. This term is considered a highly inflammatory expression of racial bigotry.*

Interestingly, the two former employees of my client begged to challenge that definition. When confronted by their supervisor about the inappropriateness of the word for the workplace they very quickly and sincerely informed him that they were friends and that they meant nothing negative by it. They went on to explain to him that that was just the way black men talked to each other.

Surprisingly, if we go back to the *DK Illustrated Oxford Dictionary* and look at their second definition for the word *nigger,* it states: *(in black English) a fellow black person.*

In essence they were all correct. The use of the word referred to in definition one is clearly inappropriate in the workplace and yet the word referred to in definition two is very commonly used amongst black young people almost as a term of endearment. What would you have done if you were the manager in this situation? What do they tell you in management training about

12

this one? We know that in the real case, the employees were terminated, but a suit was filed. Who do you think won? Could this have been handled differently without job loss or legal costs?

My second conversation was with a black female in her mid-fifties who is the senior vice president of human resources for a major corporation. She blew me away when she told me that they had just terminated three young female employees for referring to each other by the "B" word (*bitch*), "S" word (*slut*) and the "H" word (*whore* or its hip hop derivative, *ho'*). When questioned about the repeated use of the words they, like their black male counterparts at a totally separate company said it was never meant as a negative and was in fact just the way they talked to each other. They even went so far as to tell the senior VP that it was kind of like the women on *Sex and the City*. They actually referenced a television program!

More recently, I had a conversation with a middle school administrator that also shocked me. Because of the "N" word situation it didn't totally shock me, but it did cause me to make that look with my face that says, *You've got to be kidding me!* The administrator had recently interviewed a young white male for a teaching position. His collegiate transcript was solid and he had apparently done well as a student teacher, but there was one little problem. The young man who wanted to teach 6th, 7th and 8th graders had a two-inch tattoo on his neck of a marijuana leaf. What would you have done in this situation? My friend chose not to extend a job offer to the young man. He also did not mention the true reason why an offer had not been extended. Why? He didn't know whether he could legally *not* hire for that reason. What he did know was that quite a few parents of his charges would have a big problem with their 6th, 7th or 8th grader's teacher advertising an illegal drug on his neck.

Back in the mid-eighties I read an article in a business newspaper that said over 41% of the full time American workforce had their first job experience in the fast food industry. Basically, it implied that McDonald's, Wendy's, Jack-in-the-Box and Burger King taught America how to work. A couple of years ago I mentioned that article to a buddy who owns a fast food franchise. He chuckled and told me that times had changed. He informed me that at his stores he preferred to hire senior citizens for the jobs that had historically gone to teens. Why? He claimed that the teens had very little work ethic. They wanted to get paid, but they didn't want to work. He went on to say that many of them received so much cash from their parents that they didn't really need to work, so even though they expected a paycheck they did not think they should have to do the things he asked of them. In fact, he said most of them thought they should be making more money than he was paying them even though they put very little effort into their work. He said they seemed to have a sense of entitlement.

I was amazed when he said in recent years he'd had to make an official company policy about common sense things. He had to ban cell phones in the workplace because employees would get calls and answer them while customers waited. Amazing, right? Well, I'm convinced some airlines need the same policy. Earlier this week I was waiting in line to check in with an Atlanta gate agent for a flight to Montreal. Just as the last customer before me finished up, the agent's cell phone started to ring. She checked her caller id and then stooped down behind the counter to answer. (Maybe that particular airline does have a policy since she attempted to hide.) To her credit, she did tell the caller that she was working, but she stayed on the phone for at least 90 seconds. (Yes, I timed her.)

The fast food restaurant owner said his managers would often send kids out to empty the trashcans or to clean up the parking lot and then have to send someone else to see what was taking them so long. In many cases they were either on the phone or talking to friends from school who were customers. Realistically, what would you have done?

Do any of the real world scenarios I just described shock you? If they do, welcome to the club. If they don't, then we perhaps have a worse problem than I realized. Did the anecdotal comments about the jobs we used to give to kids as starter jobs surprise you? If they don't, does that also say something about our culture?

The interesting piece tied to all of this is that in every case I illustrated, the offending employees or interviewees didn't feel they had done anything wrong. I have shared these comments with kids around the country and by and large they don't seem to see what the big deal is. What do you think? The important question here is how should we handle these new world problems? Unfortunately, I am finding that my clients in the corporate world and academia have no clue of what to do.

When I started hearing stories like these I found them humorous. But then as I gave them more thought something hit me. Everything my clients described to me, I had seen before. Not necessarily in the workplace, but definitely in the halls of the more than 500 high schools I speak at annually. Yes, managers in the workplace are dealing with issues that didn't seem to exist ten or fifteen years ago. But the reality is that schools have been fighting these battles for years. Unfortunately, the American school system has not been successful in eradicating these problems and as their students have graduated and entered the workforce, so have their issues.

When I go into a middle or high school for a speaking engagement, I try to hang out in the hallway between classes and observe the kids beforehand. I hear the "N" word regularly. Even in all-white schools. I also hear the "B" word and many others. The really interesting thing is that usually there are faculty members present in the halls and in most cases this doesn't seem to impact the kids' profanity at all. The kids ignore the adults walking by and the adults do not confront the kids about their behavior.

I go into schools and I see kids with as many tattoos as Allen Iverson and as many piercings as the latest heavy metal rock star and again, no one at school comments. Whenever I mention that to parents, they always ask why the school employees don't step in and I have to tell them that they stay out of it because we as parents have taught them to stay out of it.

A few months ago, I did a session for a group of teachers in the great state of Kansas and one of the principals shared a strange scenario. She had a student who came to school dressed very inappropriately. The student wore a very low cut top that exposed her entire midsection and a pair of very short shorts.

The principal pulled the girl out of the hallway and had her put an oversized t-shirt over her clothes. A note was also sent home to her mother regarding the inappropriateness of the girl's attire. Surprisingly, the mother came to the school the next day to raise hell with the principal. She was furious. Mom accused the school of picking on her daughter. She said there was no way her daughter was the only girl dressing like that. The principal tried to get Mom to understand that the real issue was her daughter's appearance. She explained to the mother that their goal was to get kids to understand that when they get into the real work world, certain dress just would not be acceptable. The mother's response blew me away. She told the principal that in most cases she would probably be right, but that her daughter wanted to be a stripper when she grew up and in that profession, her dress would be okay. Here's the problem in America guys: I share stories like this with moms and dads in the workplace and everyone looks shocked. I share these stories with teachers and cops and there is no shock or surprise.

Who are these kids? You may want to refer to them as Generation Xers, but they are way too young for Generation X. According to Douglas Coupland, author of *Generation X,* back in 1991 the phrase *twenty-somethings* was also a very common reference to Generation Xers.

Now more than a decade later, most of those same twenty-somethings are actually thirty-somethings, but frequently the X-term is tossed in whenever there is a need for a synonym for young people. The generation we are focusing on is not made up of Xers. They are the generation just entering the workforce for the first time. They have been called a lot of things, but none of the names has really stuck like Baby Boomers or Generation X. The most common name applied to them has been The Nexters, but they have also been called Neters, Millenials, Generation Y and Generation Next. They were born between 1980 and 2000. They are more than 81 million strong—far surpassing the numbers of the Baby Boomers. They don't remember the Cold War. Watergate was just a question in U.S. history class. The world as they know it, has always had AIDS, pc's, microwave popcorn and MTV.

Over the next few chapters I will 1) identify the traits and habits of today's generation that impact their ability to be successful in the workplace; and 2) outline some of the things that as parents we will have to do to help these young people improve their probability of success.

Affording It Doesn't Mean Needing It

Congratulations parents! Based on U.S. Bureau of the Census figures, more than 50% of your kids will still be living at home with you in a dependent state until age 24. Twenty-five percent will be with their parents until they reach their mid to late thirties. When I first read these statistics I thought primarily the kids staying home would be young ladies whose over protective dads wanted to be nearby to help protect them. Wrong! Surprisingly, the majority of the young people unable to leave the nest will be male. In fact, I think we overly protective dads are worrying about the wrong thing. Many of our girls will be fine except they might end up falling in love with some sorry joker who has been living with his momma forever. His momma has been cooking for him, cleaning up behind him, supplementing his income and washing his nasty drawers for years. The scary thing is that in many cases he doesn't end up leaving his momma's home until he finds a younger woman (maybe your daughter) who is willing and able to take over his mother's job. He will then move into her apartment or house and your wallet.

Whenever I do sessions with adults I ask them, *How many of you do not want your kids living with you until they are in their mid thirties?* Every hand in the room flies up. Some parents actually moan when I share the statistics with them. With kids, I ask how many of them do not want to live with their moms or dads until they are in their mid-thirties. Their hands go up faster than the adults. The point I make to them then is that if the parents don't want the kids to stay and the kids don't want to stay and yet the statistics say they will, you must ask why. Some of the young people will yell out that they're sick of living with their parents right now.

Parents whose kids are 21 or 22 and already out of the house often break into huge grins. That is, until I tell them how many of the kids in the twenty-five percent who stay until mid or later thirties also left home. They just didn't stay. They are the Boomerang Kids— young adults who left home to go to college, get married or just be on their own who then move back in with their mom and dad. The scary part is that the numbers are increasing. So again the question is *why?*

There are numerous reasons, perhaps the biggest being finances. According to the Bureau of Labor Statistics, 10.9% of 20 to 24-year olds were unemployed in September of 2003. Compare that to 6.7% being unemployed during September of 2000. The jobless rate for 25-34 year olds practically doubled during the same time period. Some others return home because of personal problems like substance abuse, unplanned pregnancy, illness or divorce. An additional, fast growing cause that I'm hearing about from around the country is that the kids are finding that they cannot match their parents' standard of living when they first get out of school. They just can't afford the lifestyle their parents exposed them to, which isn't surprising. The reality is that I couldn't touch my parents' standard of living when I first got out of college either. My mom and dad had steaks in their freezer. I had ice cubes. The difference is that previous generations understood that they had to WORK UP to where their parents were. In speaking to a quarter million kids a year, I find that today's young people have not bought into WORKING UP to their parents' level. They want to be where their parents are— NOW!

Parents get mad at kids for feeling that way, but we have no right to. Guess who taught them to want it all right now? We did! Without meaning any harm, we taught them immediate gratification and gave them a sense of entitlement by giving and giving and giving.

It is estimated that we spend more money on kids today than any other period in American history. Think about it. I can prove it to you by just asking a couple of quick questions. Have you noticed that your kids, grandkids, nieces, nephews and godkids get more stuff on gift giving holidays like Christmas, bar and bat mitzvah and birthdays than you ever got on those occasions? Do you remember the old Sears Wish Book? It was the Christmas catalog and used to come out in October. I don't know what you did with your Wish Book, but my sisters and I would circle all the toys that we wanted. We very seldom got the stuff we circled, but we enjoyed the process. I mention the Wish Book because if you are over 35 then Sears was the number one retailer when you were a kid and sold more toys than anyone else, but think back, most Sears stores back then didn't even have a major toy section except between October and January. Why? Because in the past parents did not buy their kids toys all year long. Today, Wal-Mart is the biggest retailer in the world and they have a huge toy department seven days a week, 365 days a year. Why? They have a toy department because today's parents buy toys year round.

I remember times growing up when I might ask my mom for a toy or something. She typically had two responses: 1) No! or 2) January through March she'd tell me to write Santa Clause a letter and tell him. If I reminded her that it was only January or February and that Christmas was almost a year away, she'd tell me to write anyway and then I'd be first on his list.

Today, I ask elementary and junior high kids what they hear from their parents when they want something that is not a necessity. The responses they share with me are very different from what my sisters and I heard. What amazed me the most though was how many of them tell me they always get what they ask for. Often they giggled or out and out laughed as they told me. In the cases where their parents did not buy the trinket, the number one comment they claimed to hear was: Wait till payday. If the parents were divorced, they often heard from mom: Tell your dad. In a recent *Newsweek* article a survey of grade school children was cited that said when kids crave something new, if their mom or dad say no, the kids said their parents usually give in if they continue to ask for it. In the survey the kids even identified how many times they'd have to ask to wear their parents down. Nine times.

I grew up in a day and time when most middle class kids got new clothes twice a year: Christmas time and back to school time. It didn't matter what your religion was. Christmas time was when the big three retailers (JC Penney, Sears and Montgomery Ward) stocked up on kids' clothes. Today, we buy kids so many clothes—year round—that many parents have had the experience of going into their kid's closet or drawers and finding clothes that were purchased months earlier—never worn and price tags still on them.

If you have boys check around your house and see just how many video games—at about $38.99 to $49.99 each—they have collected over the years. Do you get what I'm saying here? Money, money, money. Now, let's not fool ourselves and say that this is just the curse of the middle and upper classes. Lower income parents are in the same boat. They just can't really afford the boat ride.

A couple of years ago I spoke in a Texas high school in a depressed economic area. The principal employer in the region had just relocated to Mexico. The school principal told me that approximately 80% of his kids were receiving government subsidized breakfast and lunch. Yet, as I walked around the gymnasium before my presentation I was amazed at how many of the kids were wearing the rather pricey Iverson sneakers by Reebok or Nikes. I also at one point asked the kids how many of them had the then just released Play Station 2 and close to 75% of the boys raised their hands.

One of the craziest things I see around America is when I go to high schools and look at the teachers' parking lot and the students' parking lot. Guess where the more expensive cars are? Without a doubt, they are in the students' lot. Now forgive me if this offends you, but I think there is something wrong in America when your snot-nosed child with no high school diploma and no college degree and no full time job is driving a nicer car than a full grown adult with a high school diploma, a college degree and a fulltime job, teaching your snot-nosed child. What message are you sending your kids? What message are you sending your teachers?

The problem with the money issues I've just described is that they lead kids to expect immediate gratification. Then when they get in college or out of college and find that they can't get every game that they want or go to every function that they want to go to, they begin to lean on credit cards. How bad is the problem? According to a study by loan provider Nellie Mae the average undergraduate leaves school with a debt of $18,900. That's a 66% increase from just five years ago. A large portion of this is of course student loans, but a growing part of this debt is unnecessary. It is tied to the immediate gratification we taught them at home. So they run up credit card debt charging pizza, t-shirts, hamburgers and beer for four years to the point that 31% of seniors leave school with credit card debts between $3,000 and $7,000.

The average college freshman will be offered eight credit cards during their first semester. The average senior has six credit cards in their name, with interest rates between 10 and 19.8%. Once they graduate things often continue to spiral. Now, if they are fortunate enough to get a job, they will probably have a car note, phone bills (home and cell), cable or satellite television bills, gas and electric bills, water/sewer bill, student loans, gasoline, food, and in many cases they go to one of those wonderful stores where you pick up furniture and don't have to pay a thing for 18-24 months. The bottom line is that in many cases they are so stretched financially that they will begin to look for an escape hatch and that will usually be mom and dad.

Now, please don't misunderstand me. By no stretch of the imagination am I saying that parents should not try to help their kids even if they are over 21. It's almost instinctual that we try to help. What I am saying though is that parents must be aware of the part we may play early on in setting our kids up for a financial fall. From my perspective, the bottom line is simply this: Just because you can afford a certain thing, doesn't mean your child needs it.

Amazingly I meet young adults who are actually doing pretty good for themselves, yet feel like failures because they can't yet match the standard set by mom and dad.

Back in the mid-nineties I had a conversation with a neighbor. He was the sole wage earner in his home and things were getting pretty tight for him. On a couple of occasions he mentioned to me that he might have to leave Atlanta in order to get promoted to the next pay grade. He and his wife loved Atlanta, their church, and home. They didn't want to leave, but he really needed the extra money. A few months later I ran into his 16-year-old son at the local grocery store driving a brand new, top of the line Mustang. The next day I asked my neighbor if he had gotten his promotion. He told me no, but he couldn't stand the idea of his son being the only starter on the high school football team without a car.

Today, his son has graduated from college, is an assistant manager at a Red Lobster, married to a wonderful young school teacher and neither he nor his wife drive a car as expensive as the car he got at sixteen. Recently, I ran into the young man in the parking lot of my local Wal-Mart.

He was driving his wife's new car. It wasn't a muscle car. It was an economy car. I liked it. I'm pretty sure it got great gas mileage. I complimented him on the car and he just kind of shrugged.

I am very proud of my neighbor's son and so are his parents, but is he proud of himself? When we give kids the world prior to adulthood, what do they have to look forward to? I really think my neighbor's son is doing okay, but he doesn't feel like a winner because it doesn't match up to what mom and dad had done for him in the past.

Unfortunately, my neighbor's son is not an exception to the rule. He might actually represent the norm. Many of the young people who do return home have also grown up in a world of excess. Some academics refer to them as the over-indulged. Now, if you are like me, when you hear that term *overindulged* you probably immediately think about the kids of the upper middle class and higher. Rich kids. But the reality is that the act of over-indulgence is prevalent on all socio-economic levels. Don't forget my experience at the school in Texas I talked about earlier.

During a speech to commemorate the fiftieth anniversary of the Supreme Court's Brown v. Board of Education school desegregation ruling, comedian Bill Cosby ripped some "lower economic" parents for "not holding up their end of the deal." "These people are not parenting. They are buying things for kids—$500 sneakers, for what? And won't spend $200 for Hooked on Phonics." Sounds like Dr. Cosby met the parents of the kids I met in Texas. Dr. James Fogarty of the American Society of Professional Education offers two distinctly different definitions of indulgence.

1. The first definition requires **access to finances**. "Parents with wealth, give to their children and do not mentor to their children. Their indulgences are severe and their lack of mentoring is severe."

2. The second definition requires no finances. "Parents, who have no wealth and no false wealth (credit cards), give their children **too much permission too soon** to do things in life that children are not prepared to handle. In other words kids have too much freedom too early. This puts children in the 'power seat' of the family, but they have no skills to manage life. In addition their parents do not mentor them."

A few years ago, I did a series of workshops with incarcerated juvenile drug dealers. The idea was to help them refocus their lives. I began each session by asking them to list what they wanted in life. Their first response was always money. I'd then follow up by asking how much money? They'd immediately reply in unison, "Big money!"

I then asked what that meant. They said, "Stupid money." I told them I still didn't know what that meant. Most of the groups finally gave me figures in the $75,000 to $150,000 a year range. I then asked them *what else?* To be honest, I thought they'd say jewelry or a car, but instead the next thing they mentioned was a house. I asked what kind of house and one of them yelled out, "A brick house!"

At that point I told him that I wasn't asking about his desire for a woman with a Coke bottle figure. They all chuckled and basically said they wanted a brick home with three or four bedrooms and baths. One of the guys yelled out that he had six sisters so he needed seven bathrooms. The next thing they wanted was a car. What type? Number one answer: a drop-top Benz (convertible). Second choice: Cadillac Escalade. After that, they picked family, which by the way, they defined as: a wife, couple of kids, and a dog. Finally, they wanted to be happy.

My response was, "Congratulations! Welcome to America." Even though society would rightfully label the drug dealers as being on the wrong side of the track in life, there was absolutely nothing wrong or sinister or corrupt about what they wanted. Those young felons wanted The American Dream. They wanted the same things that you and I want: A nice annual income, a nice home, a car, a family, health and a little happiness. Sounds like the same things you and I want for our kids. They wanted the same things that the young people working at my friend's fast food restaurant want. We all have similar dreams.

I think it would be safe to say that most of the juvenile drug dealers I work with have experienced the over indulgence described in definition two. In fact, I have found over the years that often the kids who use the most drugs are from definition one and the kids who sell dope are from definition two. Kids from strong middle- to upper-middle-class homes use about 300% more drugs than kids from low income inner city homes.

Dr. Benjamin E. Mays said it far more eloquently: *"It must be borne in mind that the tragedy of life does not lie in not reaching your goals, the tragedy lies in not having any goals to reach. It isn't a calamity to die with dreams un-filled, but it is a calamity not to dream. It is not a disaster to be unable to capture your ideals, but it is a disaster to have no ideals to capture. It is not a disgrace not to reach the stars, but it is a disgrace to have no stars to reach."*

Dreams and goals are normal and necessary. The fact that the drug dealers I met have shared American dreams is not the only thing they have in common with you and me. Like most of us, their wants and dreams are not the problem. In fact I often ask kids who are not in trouble with the law about their wants and dreams. Surprise! They want the same things the dealers want. Don't forget, the want side of the equation is basically sold to us over the airwaves. Television, radio, newspapers, mp3s, internet, movies, etc. The problem that so many of our kids run into is the *getting it* part of the equation. The drug dealers' ideas on how to realize their dreams were illegal, anti-social and held the same low probability of success as those of their law abiding peers.

Can't Your Kid
Cut the Grass?

> "I have gotten to a point
> where I just won't
> hire young people.
> They're not
> worth the trouble."
> —Casino Security Director

> "They just don't want
> to work. They want
> everything handed to them.
> I can't stand them."
> —Bank President

Something is very wrong in America. It seems that no one wants your kids. Not in the workplace at least. After hearing from the fast food restaurant owner who said he'd rather hire seniors, I started paying more attention and asking a lot more questions. At one point I mentioned the franchisee's comments to a friend at church who happens to work in the grocery business. He said he fully understood.

Apparently some managers in the grocery business have been dealing with the same problem. The only difference he could identify was that in his business they have found two types of people to replace the young people who used to bag groceries, work the cash register and retrieve shopping carts: Senior citizens and the mentally challenged. After hearing these comments I began sharing them with my audiences around the country and found that very few business people were surprised. In fact, the more I shared the comments, the more supporting anecdotes I heard.

Another former client who had been a deputy chief of police now runs security for a casino in the northeast. He heard me talk about this problem at a conference in Orlando for current and former law enforcement officials. Afterwards, he immediately came and met me before I could leave the stage area and told me that I had just described his biggest personnel problem.

Even more recently I met a woman in Alabama who is an assistant manager at the local Super Wal-Mart. After hearing my talk about nobody wanting our kids, she came up after the program to give me an example from her store. Apparently they had an 18-year-old cashier who was very fond of wearing very short mini-skirts and low cut tops. She was asked by her manager to wear longer skirts because a customer had complained that when she leaned over you could see her panties. The young lady told the assistant manager that it was her body and she could dress however she wanted. After a second conversation where the young lady again refused to adjust her attire, she was fired. Now, maybe my age is showing again here, but I just don't get it. How do you give up a job in a community that doesn't have many jobs over a mini-skirt?

Over the past five years, one of the questions I always ask parents during workshops is whether they think their kids do more or less work around the house than they did growing up. In many instances the question is greeted with chuckles, sneers and loud laughter. This again is part of the over indulgence problem. We have a group of young people whom we spend more money on than perhaps at any other time in history and that same group of young people tends to do less work around their parents' home than any other group in history. The September 13, 2004, *Newsweek* article, "The Power of No," referenced a survey in which 75% of all parents said their kids did fewer chores than children 10 or 15 years ago.

Let's think this through. We spend more money and they do less work. Try it again. *We spend more money and they do less work.* Does anything seem wrong with that equation to you? A couple of years ago I brought that equation up to a group of parents in Olympia, Washington, and they all agreed that their kids didn't do a lot of work around the house. I was interrupted by a teenager who yelled out that she washed the dishes at home. I then asked her what she washed them with. She proudly replied that her family had a Kenmore. I then politely and proudly informed her that my mom's dishwasher had a name too: MILTON. There was no dishwasher. In fact, washing dishes by hand thirty years ago was much harder than washing dishes by hand today. Back in the old days we didn't have the pots with the non-stick, Teflon surfaces and there was no such thing as PAM cooking spray. Back then it seemed that everything our mothers cooked stuck and we needed Brillo pads, steel wool, SOS pads, Comet and a good helping of elbow grease.

But the real issue is not what tools are used for working. The issue is the absence of work. Often when I discuss this issue with parents some of them seem to be mad at the kids for not working when in reality we shouldn't be mad at them. The question is, who taught them that they didn't have to work? Let me give you a hint or two. Have you ever given your kid a task to complete and then you came back later and found that either they hadn't done a thing or they did it half way or that they were just doing it in super slow motion? The times that you had that experience did these words ever creep into your conscious mind and maybe roll from your lips? *I am so tired of fooling with this kid. It would be easier for me to just do it myself and get it over with.* Now, because this is a book I don't know how you are reacting, but I can tell you this, when I ask that question in workshops, both for parent groups and in corporate settings, about 75% of the parents raise their hands and say that they have said those words. My point is simple. It probably would be easier if you did it yourself, but if you do it, what are you teaching your child? Could you be teaching them to be irresponsible? Could you be teaching them that they don't really have to do anything that they don't really want to do? Are you teaching them that others will always cover for them?

The really sad thing is that sometimes that sorry joker, that an overly indulgent parent has been raising, ends up getting a job working for someone like me and they treat us the way they treat their parents. The only problem is that we don't love them like their parents. So, if they don't do what they're supposed to do we're going to fire them. (And then they're going to move back home. And the scary part about that is some of you reading this book waited a little late in life to start having kids and you haven't figured something out. If they are going to stay with you until they are in their mid- to maybe late thirties, that may mean that they are going to stay with you until you DIE. And then they're going to take all your stuff. Now if you're okay with that fine. I'm not, my kids have got to be ready to get out of the nest and fly on their own.)

I was recently in New Jersey and met a mom who told me that about a week before my seminar she was outside cutting her family's 2- acre lawn and her 16-year-old son who had been inside playing video games came out and asked her what she would give him if he finished the lawn. She said she wouldn't give him anything and that cutting the grass was his job anyway. The boy turned around and went back inside and returned to his Play Station 2. That story amazes me every time I tell it.

Perhaps what amazes me more though is how many families I have encountered who have teenaged sons at home and they pay someone else to cut the grass. I always ask parents to explain that to me, and mothers always talk about how busy their kids are with school and sports. My question is always the same: What changed? When I was in high school, I played multiple sports, at church I was in the choir, on the usher board and an officer in the youth group. I was a boy scout, I was on student council, kept an A- grade point average, had a job at Walgreen's drug store and I still cut the grass. My question to parents is always, "Can't your kids cut the grass?"

I also find many families with teenaged boys and girls at home and mom still does most of the cooking and cleaning around the house. In quite a few cases mom is so busy that the family has to hire maid service to help mom. My, my, my how things have changed. When I was growing up my sisters and I had taken on most of the household chores before we reached our teens.

If you don't *have* to work, when do you *learn* to work? If there is never a connection between work and reward or failure and punishment, when do you learn to strive?

Is there really any wonder why so many employers will shout in unison that our young people lack work ethic? If they don't have work to do at home, when will they learn to work? Schools don't teach work ethic and aren't supposed to. That is the job of concerned parents.

Now, let's take a look at how this problem impacts the work place. I am convinced that a major part of our problem with young people today is that they have gotten almost everything their hearts desired and in most cases didn't have a lot of work to do. So, what do you think that looks like in the real world? A president of a small bank I work with in Florida put it this way:

"The young people we get in are not good workers. The work ethic just isn't there. They want to get paid. But they don't think they should have to bust their butts. I can't stand them."

I live on a 7-acre plot of land outside of Atlanta and one of my neighbors sold her 19 acres to a developer last year. He is building a subdivision with over 40 homes. There are two different contractors building the actual homes. I have gone over on the construction site a few times and talked to the job foremen. For one company the foreman is a mid-fifties white guy. The other foreman is a black guy in his mid-forties. Would you believe that every other person out there actually building the houses is Mexican? There is not one young black or young white person on the site. I asked each of the foremen about it and they both said the same thing: the American kids won't work. Period. End of story.

I shudder to think about it, but we may be living in a time and space when for many of our young people, the first time they are held accountable for their behavior and effort is when they enter the work force. The first authority figure to insist on appropriate behavior and completion of assignments is the boss. The teachers overlook the cursing and inappropriate dress. Mom buys the inappropriate dress and will defend the kid's behavior if the administration gets involved. Parents don't make the kids work and if they don't do what they are supposed to do, there's not much in terms of consequences. Does that scare you as much as it scares me?

Educators are Giving Up— On Parents

Besides the fact that many employers seem to be giving up on our young people, it also appears that many educators are giving up too—on parents. You see it really made me wonder why in the cases where the kids were using the "N" word, "B" word and others in the hallways, so often the teachers in the hall just seemed to ignore it. So, I asked. The response I got was that teachers are hesitant to intervene because in so many cases, there is no support from parents. Surprisingly, I get this feedback from law enforcement officials as well.

A few years ago I had a chance to speak to over a thousand law enforcement officers at a conference in Las Vegas. I asked them to tell me what frustrated them most in dealing with today's parents. One officer stood and told of a situation he had run into all too often. Apparently he had stopped a teen for driving under the influence, but he didn't want to arrest the kid. He decided instead to call the parents to discuss the boy's issues. The parents' response? "Not my child." The cop then told the parents that when he pulled the kid over marijuana smoke rushed out of the car window when he rolled it down. The parent's response: "Well, you know, he's got these bad friends and I'm sure they were the one's smoking the weed." The cop then said that he told the mother that her son was in the car alone. The parent's response: "I'll bet he had just let those other kids out of the car right before you pulled him over." The cop laughed and said he told the mom that the boy had admitted that it was his marijuana. The parent's response: "My son isn't 18 yet. You can't question him without me or his dad being there, or our attorney."

I then asked the rest of the audience if they had ever had similar experiences and the applause in the room was deafening. Later that same year I spoke at a conference for school administrators and I shared with them what the cops said. One of the principals stood up and told me that they see the same phenomenon. She then gave me this example: One of her teachers called a parent to tell them about some inappropriate behavior that had been displayed by their child. The parent's immediate response was: "Not my child." The teacher then reiterated to the mother what the child's behavior had been and what the school had done in response to it. The mother again claimed that her son would never do what they had accused him of doing.

The teacher, a little exasperated, then assured the mother that no one at school would make anything up about her son. The mother then told the teacher to hold on, because her son was at home and she was going to ask him. The teacher then heard the mother in the background ask the boy if he had done what they said. He denied it and the mother came back on the phone and said to the teacher, "Listen, I don't know about your children, but my children do not lie to me. My children never lie to me and my son says he didn't do it, so I know he didn't do it and I don't appreciate you calling me after I've been working on my job all day with this foolishness."

I then asked the school administrators to respond by show of hands if they had ever heard anything similar from parents in their community. Every hand in the room went up. I was amazed. Is it just me, or does that amaze you as well? My first thought was, who are these people who have children who do not lie? Children lie. Sometimes by omission and sometimes by commission, but lie they will. In fact, now when I do parent workshops if there are any teens in the room, I ask them a few questions about telling all, part or none of the truth. The first question I ask the kids is: How many of you have told your parents something before that was not quite the truth? Every teen hand in the room goes up. I then ask them if they've ever taken the time to think their lie out before telling their parents. The kids usually start laughing as about 80% raise their hands. Then I ask them if they've ever bounced their lie off one of their friends to see if it sounded believable. After another round of laughter, about 60% raise their hands. Then I ask them my favorite question: How many of you have ever told your parents such a big lie and when they bought it, you actually had to go in another room to laugh? Easily, 40% of the kids raise their hands. In other words, mom and dad, not only have our kids lied to us, but they have even laughed at us as well.

The bottom line is that kids do lie. That is reality. Now, here is the good news. Your kid lying to you does not necessarily make your child a bad child. It also does not make you a bad parent. Your child lying to you and you letting them get away with it without following up or checking up on them can make your child an irresponsible child who grows up to be an irresponsible adult.

The best way I can phrase the situation is that it appears that in today's environment we have more parents covering for their kids instead of correcting their kids when there's a problem. The end result of that is that then when there are issues at school, a lot of educators take a hands-off approach because they feel they will not get the support of parents. Think about the story I shared with you earlier of the mother who said her daughter wanted to be a stripper.

As weird and frustrating as this may seem, it kind of comes down to the new American phenomenon of parents who have decided that they would rather be their child's best friend instead of their parent. Why? It's simply because parenting is hard work. Most of you have no idea how often I get parents after programs who tell me that they just don't have a parent-child relationship with their kids. Instead, they are like *best friends.* For those of you who think like that, my comment to you is simple. If you are 44, and your best friend is 12, something is wrong. Either that is the most mature child known to man or you are a little slow, and personally, I'm betting on the child being normal. As parents, we need to teach our kids socialization skills so that they can meet, make and keep good friends. A 12-year-old kid's best friend should be 12 or 13 at most. A 40-year-old adult's best friend should be around 40. This ain't rocket science, folks. It's good, old-fashioned common sense.

My father and I are great friends today, but when I was a kid growing up, Billy, Reggie and Cliff were my friends. Daddy was daddy. Sometimes my daddy was the enemy, because he often kept me from doing the things I wanted to do. The amazing part though is that I don't think my daddy cared whether I considered him an enemy or a friend.

So why are so many parents concerned today? I think there are three primary reasons why parents today want to be their children's friends. Now, just as a point of clarification, it's important to understand that these parents have not chosen to be their kid's best friend *instead* of their parent. No. Absolutely not. What they want is to be their child's best friend and their parent. Unfortunately folks, we don't have that luxury. During the formative years, the roles of parent and friend are so diametrically opposed that it is very hard to walk in both shoes. Parents have to make tough decisions and set boundaries that kids just won't like or understand. (And they're not supposed to!)

Now, as I stated earlier, I have found in parent workshops that adults want to be best friends for three basic, guilt-based reasons:

1. Divorce: I meet numerous parents who feel as though their failed marriage has injured their child so much that they have to somehow make up for it. Too often making up for it simply means never setting boundaries or limits for the child. In essence the child becomes the boss of the house. You can't make up for a broken family with broken parenting. Parents don't realize that in reacting to a divorce, which is more common today than uncommon, they may actually be sentencing their child to a lifetime of unfulfilled dreams.

2. Schedules: The reality of life in this new millennium is that most families need two incomes. As a result, today's parents put in more hours on the job and at the end of a long, tiring work week, it's tempting and easier to buy peace with yes and go along with the child's wants, rather than tie up rare family time with conflict. I meet many parents who feel so bad about their schedules and the amount of time they spend away from their families that they refuse to let any of their limited family time be negative. They want all interactions with their kids to be about fun, games, going out to dinner and such. Unfortunately, what they miss is that if their time with their kids is limited, then they can't miss opportunities to teach kids the right things. When you think about it, our primary responsibility as parents is to prepare our children to be able to take care of themselves.

3. We Can't Be Our Parents: It never ceases to amaze me when I do parent programs to hear so many parents (mothers especially) comment about all the things that their mothers did, that they just aren't able to do. From the cooking of fresh meals almost daily, to the cleaning and anything else imaginable. One of the first things I try to tell parents is to take a reality check. First of all, our parents were not perfect parents. They did the best they could with the information at hand. Just like you and I. There was no instruction book for raising kids when your folks started either. The truth is that there are some things your parents did well and others they didn't. Your mom may have cooked a lot of meals, but first of all, it wasn't because she wanted to. If she had the modern conveniences that you have she would have used them. Secondly, your mom and dad lived in a much simpler time, and in a much simpler world than you do. Most of our parents were raised with— and tried to raise us with—the values of thrift, self sacrifice and hard work. As a result we heard "no" a lot, had strict boundaries regarding behavior and had lots of chores to do. Many of today's young parents swore that they would never do what their parents did. They swore to have closer relationships with their kids and to let their kids participate in decision-making and not to set so many boundaries. As we've gotten older though, many of us now see the value in some of the things our parents did and we long for the good old days. We want our kids to respond to certain stimuli the way we did, but they haven't had the same experiences. So stop beating yourself up because you can't do everything your mom did. Especially, don't then become this non-parent to your child because you don't think you can be the mom that your mom was. I find that my mom and dad look at my schedule and my sister's and say they have no idea how we survive. My parents are good people and they were great parents for my sisters and me, but they were far from perfect. My sister Cyde and I have often discussed the fact that we don't remember our parents spending a whole lot of time helping us with our homework. Today's mom and dad have to do homework duty. I don't recall my dad making it to any of my high school athletic contests. He was busy working, but today's parents will race from work to make it to the game.

If you, like me, do not want your kids living with you until they are in their late thirties, then you must do your job. If you want your kids to be able to get and keep a good job that allows them to be independent and a productive member of our society, then you must do your job. You must be a parent. When they are wrong, don't cover for them or protect them. You must correct the behavior. When teachers, cops, youth leaders, mentors, counselors and youth pastors are trying to help your child, you need to help them.

Everyday Foolishness

Earlier today I was in my father's favorite store—Wal-Mart. My plan was to run in and return a pair of shoes I had picked up for my youngest daughter that didn't fit and get out. But I got stuck in the customer service area watching a young mother deal with a tantrum of the highest order performed by her three or four-year-old son. Normally, in the customer service area they have shopping baskets full of merchandise waiting to be returned to the shelves. While waiting for his mother, the young man had found a toy in one of the carts that he wanted. His mother told him no and it was as though she had turned a switch on. First he started with a little light whining and begging where he said, "Please momma," a lot. I watched as both the mother and the lady waiting on her began to chuckle a little. They thought he was cute. Then he quickly escalated to crying. From there he went to screaming and stomping his foot. No one was chuckling then but me and I was trying to hide it.

Whenever I see outbursts like that two thoughts hit me: 1) Couldn't the momma tell what was going to happen? I could. 2) My kids have never done stuff like that. I'm sure the momma had a slight clue of what might be about to happen, but I guess she was practicing the Oh Lord technique. You know the Oh Lord technique don't you? It's the one where mom or dad is watching the child's behavior escalate and deep inside they're praying, "Oh Lord, please don't let that child lose his mind in this store." I learned about the Oh Lord technique from a guest I had on a television series I did some years ago for PBS called *Parenting Works!* It was a talk show for parents of pre-school children that looked at how to handle some of the common problems we all run into. I was amazed during every episode to hear of some of the things many of the parents were going through. Many of their problems were not common to my experiences with my kids. Thank goodness.

Probably the most memorable example for me was when one mom from Denver talked about her son throwing a tantrum at Wal-Mart after she would not buy him a particular toy. The boy first cried and stomped his feet, which mom ignored. The boy then threw himself on the floor and wailed and kicked his feet. The mother's response was to get on the floor next to him and wail and kick her feet as well. She said that he then stopped wailing and got up and told her to get up too. Well, apparently that worked for that mom, but I don't think that would have been my solution. Hell, forget the solution piece, I don't think any of my kids would have ever tried me like that.

For years, I have been referred to on the speaking circuit as the parenting guy because so much of my work has been in that area. Not only the PBS series, but also a couple of video based training programs for parents, *Parent to Parent* to help parents keep their kids away from substance abuse and *Parenting is the Key*. I do believe that parenting is the key and that parenting does indeed work, but it must be done. Part of the problem I see nationwide is that all too often kids begin doing inappropriate things at a very early age and parents find it cute or funny. The truth of the matter is that sometimes kids do things that are funny or cute, but they still need to be corrected or reprimanded— and you can't do it with a grin on your face.

A few years ago when my youngest daughter was four, she, her nine-year-old sister, and I had brunch at my sister's house. After we finished the girls wanted to go out to play in the front yard. One of the nine-year-old's best friends was a neighbor and was already out playing. While helping my sister clean up, we heard a huge crash and ran to the front door. My eldest and her friend were standing in the front yard staring towards the driveway with their mouths open. I quickly followed their gazes to the driveway and started looking for my little one. What I saw instead of my four-year old, was my car which had somehow rolled from the downward-sloped driveway into and through my sister's garage door. Fear tore through me when I couldn't see my four-year old anywhere. Then I saw her. She was sitting in the car, in the back seat where she normally sits with her seat belt on and her hands clasped neatly in her lap. I ran over and asked her if she was okay. With a very tight grin on her face she looked over at me and said very quickly, "Sorry." The way she said it broke the tension. In fact the way she said it was hilarious. My sister slipped back in the house so that she could laugh. I wanted to laugh as well, but I could not. I quickly got my daughter out of the car and swatted her fanny three quick times and sent her in the house.

The fact of the matter is that my daughter's driving experience has become one of those stories in the family that won't ever die. The child got behind the steering wheel and took the car out of park and put it in drive. (Which I didn't know could be done without a key, but apparently in a 1990 Jaguar it can.) Then after hitting the garage door, she had the presence of mind to get out from behind the wheel and get in the backseat where she belonged and to put on her seat belt and attempt to look innocent.

The whole incident was funny, but as a parent I couldn't afford to let my child think it was cute because she could have been seriously hurt and she could have really hurt someone else.

By no stretch of the imagination am I saying that we can't have fun with the things our kids do, but things that can become aberrant behavior later must be addressed. A couple of years before the car incident my little one was sitting in church with me and during his sermon the pastor started repeatedly asking a rhetorical question. It was something along the lines of, "Who told you that you aren't good enough?"

After about his sixth or seventh time of yelling out the question, Alexis looked up from her coloring book and yelled back, "I did!" Everyone sitting around us broke into laughter. The pastor even stopped to look to see who had answered him. He chuckled too. I reached over and shushed her, and later I tried to explain a rhetorical question to her, but there was no spanking or timeout or anything disciplinary.

My sister Cyde and I were seated next to a couple of young mothers and their three preschool kids recently at a local restaurant. The kids were making such a commotion that at one point I asked my sister if my kids had ever acted like that. She quickly said no and added that the kids next to us were not restaurant ready. I chuckled. A little later the two mothers were smiling and making kiddie noises at the one little girl at the table who was now trying to explain to the lady who wasn't her mom, what she learned in dance class. Then the little girl stood up in her chair to demonstrate a move. The mothers kept smiling and giggling. (I guess it was cute.) They smiled and giggled right up to the point when the little girl fell off the chair. Thank goodness she landed mostly on her left shoulder and not her head. Thank goodness she didn't hit her head on the table on the way down. Thank goodness she didn't fall onto the table and maybe break one of the glasses on the table on her way. Thank goodness she was a lucky kid, since her mother was too busy finding her inappropriate behavior cute to protect her.

Parenting does work, but it must be done. My 12-year-old and I have little run-ins on a regular basis regarding what she considers appropriate dress and what I consider appropriate. Just this past weekend, the family was getting ready to go to dinner at a very nice up-scale restaurant. She came out of her room in a pair of jeans with a long, wrinkled white tee shirt and some flip-flops with a big white flower on them. I sent her back to her room to change and I think I caught a glimpse of her rolling her eyes as she headed back. She came back five minutes later dressed very appropriately. Clearly, she knew how she should have dressed because no one had to go in and help her choose an outfit. She had a slight attitude as we headed for the garage and so I told her that she had an option: She could stay home and I could save some money. The attitude went away and we all had a great time and a great meal. My daughter needed to learn from her parents that what might be appropriate for one environment is not automatically appropriate for another. How might it have impacted the decision making of the young lady who was canned from Wal-Mart for wearing her mini-skirts if her parents had made it clear that you can't just wear what you want wherever you go?

Is This
Your Kid?

A couple of years ago during the Christmas holidays I stopped at a gas station in Atlanta. While filling my tank I heard someone calling my name. It was a young man of maybe 24 or 25 years of age. I didn't recognize him and wondered how he knew me. He said he'd heard me speak at his high school six or seven years earlier. I was flattered that he remembered me. Even more so that he remembered my name. He worked at the gas station. He had just finished cleaning the outside restrooms when he saw me. "I remember everything you told us," he said as he swept the grounds around the pumps. "I just didn't believe life would be this hard."

From what he shared with me I realized that he'd heard one of the talks I do for high school kids that focus on staying away from drugs and making decisions that don't rob your future. I asked him what he'd thought he'd be doing with his life by now. He gave me an embarrassed chuckle when he said, "Not this."

He further shared that life hadn't appeared so hard on television and that life with his parents had also seemed simple. Though his parents were hard workers they struggled. Yet, despite their struggles they managed to spoil him. They told him that his job was to go to school. Everything else, they handled. His mom cleaned his room, washed his cloths and cooked his meals. They had a lawn service. He just went to school and hung out with his friends. I'm sure he had teachers and relatives who, like me told him to get himself together and be prepared to work hard, but he didn't get it. Too bad he didn't get a slice of reality ten or twelve years earlier.

Finally after a few minutes of conversation and my questioning, he said that he had initially dreamed of going to college and becoming a computer graphics designer. He also said he'd had a girlfriend and had hoped they would have married by now. So, what were his goals or dreams?

1) Go to college.
2) Graduate from college.
3) Become a graphics designer.
4) Marry his high school sweetheart.
5) Enjoy life!

Wonderful goals! Just like the drug dealers, he had solid dreams for his life. Standing in front of the gas station, he seemed like a nice kid. Unlike most drug dealers, this young man grew up in a nice suburban community with two parents in the home who supported and encouraged his goals and dreams. But like the drug dealers, his problem was attainment of the dreams. He didn't have a clue.

I had a good friend in college whom I admired greatly. To be honest I was jealous of her. In four years of college she got two new cars. She always had money and probably was the best dressed person on campus. There was nothing her parents wouldn't give her. This young lady and I actually dated for a while and I never understood why with all the advantages her folks gave her that she was so lazy. Most of our arguments were about her not getting up on time for classes. It just didn't make sense to me. She was beautiful, intelligent and classy, but something was missing.

Since our undergrad days, she has dropped out of law school, never stayed on a job for more than a year and a half. Amazingly, no matter how many times she loses jobs, people will always hire her, because in an interview she is so impressive. She wants the finer things in life and is convinced that she deserves them, but she has never been willing to bust her butt to get them. (Thank God I never married her.)

Today, at 44 years of age, she and her daughter and her daughter's child all live with and basically on her mother. The last time I saw her mother, she said she just didn't understand where she went wrong. I do. By the way, if you'd asked my friend when we were in college, she would have told you that her mom was her best friend.

What went wrong in these two cases? Actually, a lot. Both of these young people had parents who were of that new breed of parent that prefers being their child's friend moreso than their parent. Believe it or not folks, there are some truisms in life and one is that parenting is not a popularity contest. Parents have to make the hard calls and then stick with them—even when it's easier to give in. Parents have to demand performance, even when it's easier to do it yourself. Parents have to learn to say NO and mean it! Parents have to often say the same things over and over and over again. When parents do that, kids consider us an annoying pain in the butt, which isn't necessarily a bad thing.

Back in the mid-seventies America went through its first big push for seat belts. A number of government agencies and non-profits flooded the media with hard cold facts. They talked about how many lives could be saved and how many injuries could be avoided or minimized. They talked about lower insurance premiums and protecting children. Surprisingly, the media crush accomplished very little. When seat belts were universally put in cars approximately 15% of the public used them. After the media crush, usage went up to 16%. The researchers then decided that a new form of seat belt persuasion was needed: Attractive extrinsic incentives to riders who buckle up. The logic was that if people don't buckle up voluntarily, then maybe an attractive incentive would change their behavior.

Some colleges tried sweepstakes where the campus police collected tag numbers of people using their seatbelts and the tag numbers were then entered into a weekly raffle for prizes valued from $20 to $450. They put up numerous posters advertising the campaign and the campus radio station pushed the program. At one Virginia university the campaign was considered a success because seat belt usage went up from 16.6% to 25.8%. Yet maybe it was a failure also, sent still 75% of the population was not using seat belts.

Since the attractive incentive didn't really work, by 1984 almost all automobiles have featured aversive stimuli to get people to use their seat belts. Most automobiles today feature at least an annoying buzzer that continues until the driver fastens his seat belt. Guess what the research shows? The annoying buzzer works. For drivers with intact, aversive stimulus systems, seat belt usage was 100% with the annoying, pain in the butt buzzer. Which again, isn't necessarily a bad thing.

I really don't understand parents not pushing their kids today. Mediocrity is not an option when the middle class is shrinking.

Earlier in this chapter we looked at a couple of kids that most of us would not want to claim as ours. Not because they are or were bad kids, it's just that they were misguided kids and in most cases misguided by parents who meant no harm, but did great harm. Now, don't go thinking it is all doom and gloom, because it's not. The truth is that parenting does work, but remember, you've got to do it.

A few weeks ago I was reminiscing with my sister and niece about when my oldest sister, Gail was still alive. One thing was always a given if you went to Gail's house was that it was going to be immaculate. No dirty dishes in the sink, everything in its place, no trash waiting to be taken out, no bed unmade. My sister was a wonderful housekeeper. Well, in the middle of me going on and on about my sister's housekeeping skills, my niece Jennifer (Gail's daughter) jumped in. "Momma's house was always clean, but let's not be confused about how it got that way," she told me. "Momma never even made her own bed from the time I turned 10. She'd call me in and ask me to make it for her. From about twelve I cleaned the whole house cause I didn't want to hear her mouth. I also had to keep my grades up if I didn't want to hear it. So I did." I couldn't help but chuckle as I listened to my niece. I'm sure she got tired of hearing my sister's mouth, but I'm glad my sister ran her mouth. My niece didn't have the luxury of moving back in with her mom, because her mom passed while she was in college. The good news though is that my niece (who did not get a car in high school, did not get very much more for Christmas than her mother, my other sister and I, who had to work around the house even though she was an athlete, who eventually went to college on a volleyball scholarship) got the message from her mom. The message was clear, *it is hard out there and mediocrity will not cut it.* Today, my niece has her master's degree, is married to a wonderful young man who is currently working on his master's. They have already bought their first home and Jennifer has been promoted on her job three times in two years. If you ask my niece she'll tell you that her mom was not her best friend growing up. In fact, she'll tell you that sometimes her momma seemed like the enemy. But she appreciates the way her mom raised her. Me too.

Sitting in the barbershop the other day I ran across an interesting article in the Atlanta newspaper about a Georgia Tech football player, P.J. Daniels. His mom and dad split up when he was very young. Living with his mom, he found that she was the one who overlooked it when he broke the rules. "When I stayed with my mother, she showed me all the unconditional love you can receive from any human being. She nurtured me," Daniels said. "Then I started getting out of control. I was really getting out of hand, I could have been put in jail, killed, whatever."

P.J.'s father who immigrated to the United States from Ghana, then said, I think it's time he stays with me. P.J. says his dad was incredible. When he first got there the rules were simple: Go to school, come home, no phone calls, eat and study. "It was kind of like prison to me, man. But, that's the African life," P.J. says. "You've got to obey the father." I don't think P.J. considered his father his best friend back then. He probably thought he was the enemy. Also, I don't think his father cared whether P.J. thought they were friends.

Listen to his father's comments: *I am very strict. I tell my son that if you do good, society will hold you up. If you do wrong, society will bring you down. In our tribe, the firstborn son means a lot to us. It is up to the father to make sure he leads a good life. His mom used to say to me, "Why are you so strict with him? Why can't he hang out with his friends?" I told her, I don't give a damn about his friends. His friends don't pay the bills. When P.J. wondered why I was so strict I used the tree analogy. When you plant a tree in your yard, you want it to shade the house. But it's going to grow where it wants, so you have to stake the tree down so that it grows straight to fulfill its purpose.*

Today, P.J. Daniels is one of the best running backs in the college ranks and an academic All-American at one of the tougher universities in the country. I think he is growing straight to fulfill his purpose.

One of my heroes is a young man I met a few years ago. He was one of a group of students who were being recognized for finishing the Morehouse College and Georgia Tech Dual Degree Engineering Program. I was the keynote speaker for the event. Calvin was a unique kid who originally aspired to be a professional basketball player and from what I understand, he was an exceptional high school player. He fully expected basketball to carry him through college and life. Unfortunately, Calvin severely separated his shoulder in a high school game and never regained his old form.

Calvin still knew he needed to go to college, but he didn't know how he'd do it. Nobody seemed to want him now that basketball was gone. His SAT scores weren't what they should have been. His parents, particularly his mom wouldn't let him give up. His mom had always pushed him. Not only was he a star athlete in high school, but he also had loads of household responsibilities and chores.

He decided to major in engineering because someone told him he could make good money. Unfortunately, none of the engineering schools he applied to wanted him. Finally, one little school in Georgia—Morehouse—offered him a conditional entrance. In other words, he was on probation. They'd let him in and watch him during his first semester. Thankfully, he survived that first semester.

During his undergrad years, his mother got very sick and Calvin wanted to go home and be with her. She told him to stay there and finish what he'd started. His mom later passed. Calvin did finish what he started. He received two bachelor's degrees from Morehouse and a master's and doctorate from Georgia Tech in Electrical Engineering. Calvin will tell you that his parents were hard on him and had no interest in being his buddy. He'll also tell you that today, he's so glad they did it the way they did.

When I was a freshman football player in college, like most of my teammates I dreamed of playing in the NFL one day. My coach told us that only the pure in heart would make it to the pro level. Coach Moore said that every play, we had to *want* it more than the guys we lined up against. Initially, I took him literally, but then I got it. He wanted us to know that even though there were no guarantees, if making it to the next level was truly our goal there were certain *things* we would have to do. We couldn't just want it. He was talking about a level of commitment and effort. Mediocrity was not an option.

Later in my collegiate career I met a young lady and fell in love. I don't mean that "Oh, I really like her" kind of love. No, I fell in that, "Oh my God, where have you been all my life?" kind of love. She was beautiful and charming so it should come as no surprise that I wasn't the only guy on campus interested. My coach's words came racing back to me. I had to want it more than the guys I was lined up against. In other words, there were certain things I would have to do to capture her heart. I would have to be pure in heart. Again, it was about a level of commitment and effort. Mediocrity was not an option.

Everyday I walk through malls, airports, restaurants, stores and fast food joints and see people working who look miserable and I wonder what were their dreams when they were sixteen? I doubt if any of them said, "I want to work the fry station when I'm 28," or "I'd love to clean public toilets at the gas station on the corner." So what happened? What were they committed to? What was their effort level? I bet the parents of the young man at the gas station wonder just like my old girlfriend's mom: What happened? According to the young man who does clean the toilets at the gas station, three things messed him up.

1) Television depicted real life. He always thought making it would be easy because it looked easy on television and it seemed easy in his parent's home. I must confess that when he mentioned that making it looked easy on television I actually wanted to laugh. My mind was having a hard time grasping that someone might mistake a scripted program for real life. Then again I had a hard time believing that three young ladies using the "B" word would reference a tv show when questioned by their company's human resources director, but they did. As I gave it more thought I realized that television producers and directors go to great lengths to make art look like real life. The American Academy of Pediatrics says that the average American child sees more than 40,000 commercials a year. In those commercials people are basically getting what they want (the product) and it never looks difficult. We won't even talk about the television shows where people working very basic jobs are living much better than they possibly could in real life. Add to that the big mistake that most middle class parents make when they hide hard times from their kids, thereby denying them the opportunity to learn real life experiences.

It's almost as though we are ashamed of the hard work we've had to put into making it. I think this happens partly because so many parents get caught up in the images our kids have of us when they are little. We are right up there with superheroes to them. I recently had a short stay in the hospital due to an allergic reaction to medication a doctor had prescribed. One of my daughters cried when she saw me in the emergency room because I looked really sick. She said that Daddy wasn't supposed to be sick like that. My girls are seven and twelve. To them I am a Captain America kind of guy. It is a real hero worship kind of thing. Who wants to change that image by letting them know just how hard we are fighting to keep our heads above water? So, we do anything and everything we can to make sure our children have access to all the things we did not.

2) School was a dress rehearsal. He always thought when he was goofing off in school that he could get it together later. For some reason in America we seem to operate with a mindset that says we have all the time in the world. It's as though we haven't figured out that time is the one resource that we can neither buy nor produce more of. The supply that each of us has is set in stone. Oh yes, we sometimes talk about making up time or saving time, but the reality is that time keeps right on ticking off and we cannot create it or reserve it. We can't remix it, replay, reverse, rewind, resend or resuscitate it. The only thing we can do is use it wisely.

3) The red carpet parties would never end. He was so busy being the life of the party and having fun that he never really took the time to work on his dreams. He figured they would work themselves out. The reality of life is that nothing just happens. Things don't just work themselves out. We have to work them out. We have to make things happen. I am convinced that too often we spend so much time on things that add nothing to the quality of our lives that we are clearly setting ourselves up for disappointment.

Bottom Line: The young man had great goals but his ideas on how to realize his dreams had an incredibly low probability of success. We can probably agree that, he didn't do the things he needed to do. My old coach would have said that the attendant was not one of the pure in heart. During our short time at the gas station, that young man helped me answer a question Langston Hughes asked in a famous poem: What happens to a dream deferred?

Dream Deferred

What happens to a dream deferred?
Does it dry up
Like a raisin in the sun?
Or fester like a sore—
And then run?
Does it stink like rotten meat?
Or crust and sugar over—
like a syrupy sweet?
Maybe it just sags
like a heavy load.

Or does it explode?

I am convinced that deferred dreams will not just go away. They stick around and tease at the corners of our minds and make our spirits sag. The young gas station attendant carried a very heavy load called regret that festered on him like a never-healing sore.

It Doesn't
Just Happen

Obviously, the young man we looked at in the previous chapter didn't get into the mess he's in overnight. It was a long, long process— probably, lifelong. It is critical that he accept responsibility for his situation and do something about it, but the truth of the matter is that he didn't create this quagmire by himself.

A couple of years ago during a trip back to my old neighborhood in Chicago, one of my childhood friends who is repeatedly in and out of drug rehab and lives in his parents' basement asked me to give my dad a message. He said that he wished his parents had been as hard on him as my dad had been on my sisters and me. I nearly passed out.

The message is clear. The Bible puts it another way: "Train up a child in the way he is to go, so that when he is old he will not depart from it." In other words mom and dad, if we don't do our part early in our children's development, it will be almost impossible for them to do their part.

Perhaps, the ironic part about my friend sending my dad a message was that when we were kids, I wished my parents could be more like his. I thought he and the rest of my friends had it made. I always had more work to do. They could always stay outside later than my sisters and I. We had to be in the house when the streetlights came on. My friends fooled around in school. I was expected to get A's. Most of the kids on my block didn't even cut their family's lawn. Their fathers did. I heard more lectures, had more restrictions, less freedom, and even though I always had a job and they never did, I always had less money.

I remember in high school, a friend's mom told him and me that if we wanted to have sex with a girl, we could bring her to their house and do it there. She said she knew boys were going to be boys and she didn't want us trying anything at some girl's house and get caught by her father who might try to hurt us. I thought she was the coolest of the cool. Her son could do almost anything he wanted and it was cool. My opinion of my buddy's mom has changed as I have grown up. She was not the coolest of the cool. But she just might have been the dumbest of the dumb.

While hosting *Parenting Works* I became convinced that all too many parents tend to be extremists. On one end are those who seem to allow their children to do whatever they want, whenever they want and however they want. Then there are those who don't want their kids to do anything. They over protect their kids and attempt to make all of their decisions for them.

During a parenting session in northern Quebec a while back, a couple of pre-school kids came in with their dad and sat on the front row. Ten or fifteen minutes into the session the two kids got up and came on stage with me and started playing on the stage. The father never moved and never said a word. I tried to keep going, but the father acted like he hadn't noticed that his kids were on the stage, performing. A lot of the other adults seemed to be dividing their attention between the dad and me, waiting to see what he was going to do. Finally after twelve minutes of sharing the stage with my co-stars I stopped and told them to get off the stage. They did what I told them, but the father still never said a word. A few minutes later they were up raising hell again. But they did not come back on my stage. Instead they attacked the refreshment table that the client had set up. Of course the plan was for refreshments to be served after the program. Within minutes cookies were on the floor and the little urchins had left their fingerprints on just about everything on the table. And I bet you guessed it, the father did not say or do a thing.

My point to parents is that if you set no limits for your child, what chance does a teacher have when they are trying to maintain control in the classroom? While on the same trip to Quebec I was invited to go into the bush to fish with a family. We went to a traditional Cree Nation campground a few kilometers from Waskaganish on the Rupert River. We fished near some of the most beautiful rapids you could imagine. To get there we drove to a small dock and then went by boat to the rapids. On the way there the daughter of one of my friends, Thomas Hester, the local Youth Chief was playing with a piece of plastic that she had pulled off of a grocery bag. After the plastic lost its attraction, she held it over the side of the boat and was about to drop it in when her father spoke up in a loud, stern, no nonsense voice. Because he was speaking in his native Cree tongue, I can't be certain what he said, but I've got a good idea. As soon as he spoke, his daughter pulled her arm back into the boat and sat the piece of plastic down on the floor of the boat. Had her father been like the man at my session the plastic and anything else that the child had wanted to throw would now be polluting the mighty Rupert.

On the other end of the spectrum I often run into parents who will start to yell and scream at their kids for the least little infraction. In fact I have a few cousins who operate like that all the time. The big problem with that is that the kids become so used to the screaming that after a time it has no impact. It becomes their norm. For the father to sit and say nothing while his kids were disrupting a formal meeting was absolutely wrong, but it would have been equally wrong for him to start yelling, screaming and generally creating more of a scene than his kids. Riding on the river, mere yards from dangerous rapids, my friend Thomas did not yell or scream, but his displeasure with his daughter's behavior was clear.

My father would not have made a scene, but he would not have allowed my sisters or me to behave like that. Keep in mind that the silent father's behavior I saw in Quebec was extreme and the yelling I see and hear from some of my family members is also extreme, but we don't have to be extremists to help our kids get the message. I have a good friend in Atlanta whose company I honestly enjoy. He is my fraternity brother and we have known each other for close to twenty years. We often play pool together at my house, yet there have been numerous occasions when I have wanted to invite him over for a game, but didn't. Even though he and I have kids who are around the same age, I am sometimes reluctant to invite him because he will probably bring his son. He is not as bad as the father in Quebec, but close.

My children understand that there is a difference between adult activities and family activities. His do not. On more than one occasion I have said to his son that children do not play on my pool table and yet he continues to come into the room where his father and I are playing asking if he can play. Sometimes he will just pick up a cue and approach my table. His dad usually says a very weak, "I'll teach you later." On one occasion while I was in the kitchen getting something to drink his dad let him shoot on my table. My kids know very well that if daddy is entertaining adults in the billiard room, they are not to come in unless they need to ask or tell me something. My buddy seems to be unable or unwilling to tell his kids no, unless they have made him very angry because their bad behavior has escalated. At that point he shifts to the opposite extreme of yelling or hitting.

In the animal kingdom, the mature animal initially brings food for their young. But then as time goes by carnivores begin to take their young on the hunt with them and herbivores take their young on foraging expeditions. Why? They do it because they instinctively know that at some point the young ones will have to be able to take care of themselves and their own young.

Compare that with what we have been doing in the human kingdom over the last twenty years or so. We provide the necessities of survival for our young when they are babies just like in the animal world. The problem though is that unlike the lion and lioness in the jungle, we don't stop. We usually go beyond the necessities and provide all of their wants as well because we never had those things and because we can afford them. We pick them up when they fall. We cover for them when they are in the wrong.

Today, many parents don't even want their kids to stumble, fall or fail at play. So guess what we've done? Parents have taken charge of kids' playtime activities. Which again is fine when they are very, very young. When I was a kid on the south side of Chicago, I couldn't wait to get home from school. My routine was the same everyday. I'd run home and get my homework done as quickly as possible and then I'd get outside to play with my friends as fast as my legs would carry me. If we had enough people we'd play softball. If not we'd play basketball, tag, hide-and-seek, red rover, four square, running bases, volleyball, or a number of other games. None of this was done at a park or rec center, it was all done in the street in front of our houses. Every so often we'd stop to let cars go by, but none of us ever got hit by a car. The really cool thing was that the kids decided what to play. We picked the teams. We interpreted the rules. We policed those who didn't want to play by the rules or who cheated or played too rough. We gave each other tips on how to get better. We played so much that everyday, you won and you lost. So when we won we never got too high and we lost we never sank too low. Everyday we had a chance to redeem ourselves.

Today when kids play they are usually driven to a park or ball field by parents. Once there, they are handed over to another adult who tells them what team they are on, teaches them to play, tells them how long they will play, monitors their play, interprets the rules and resolves all conflicts. Then in amazement we wonder why when kids are 14 or 15 years old, schools have to try to teach them conflict resolution and many of them are suffering from depression, anxiety and what Hara Estroff Marano in *Psychology Today* calls a psychological fragility.

No doubt, we need to take care of our kids when they are young, but we must also make sure we are teaching them the things they will need to know when they become the adults and have to take care of their young. We cannot do everything for them, give everything to them and shield everything bad from them. Human beings, like animals learn from trial and error—adjustment—and then additional trial and error.

Believe it or not, this is the most important chapter of this book. All of the preceding chapters identified the problem. The remaining pages are the *So What?* section. In a nutshell it is the part of the book that addresses the question, *Okay, we know what's going on, so what do we do?*

This is also the toughest part of the book. Not because the solutions are that complicated to identify. In fact they're pretty obvious. You see, if part of the problem is that we spend so much money on our kids that they are completely sold on immediate gratification, then obviously part of the solution is to simply stop. Cease and desist! Just say no!!!

The difficulty is that we are creatures of habit and our spending patterns are a part of our routine. We have repeated them so often that they have become deep-seeded habits. In other words we do it not based on a conscious thought or decision. It is rote, below consciousness, repetitive, habitual behavior. Again, the solution is not that hard to figure out—just hard to do. Change our habits. Please notice I said change them, not eliminate them. Think of it as replacing them with more effective ones.

My friends I mentioned earlier all developed bad, ineffectual habits. None of them finished college and ended up living with their parents or older siblings in a dependant state as adults. One flunked out of Middle Tennessee State University and lived with his mother until she died. Today he's still fighting a battle with cocaine. Another of my friends still lives in a room in his deceased parents' basement. His sister lives upstairs with her family and maintains the house. He too is fighting cocaine addiction and alcohol. My third buddy also flunked out of college, but not before getting a girl pregnant whom he then fought for custody of the baby because he didn't want to pay child support. After winning custody he promptly dropped the kid off with his parents for them to raise.

The scary part is that as a kid, I admired all of these guys. One was the best natural athlete I knew. Another was an only child who got everything. Every toy, every bit of cool gear—car, clothes, jewelry, stereo, television—he got it. The third guy I mentioned to you got all the goodies too—and freedom of movement that I couldn't even imagine. I thought they had it made!

Consistently, I share with parents that our primary responsibilities are to make sure that our kids leave the nest with four key traits: responsibility, accountability, dependability and maturity. Unfortunately, if our kids are like we were as kids they actually want more freedom, money, cool gear and to be left alone. In other words they want to live like my buddies did. I can't blame them. I wanted to live like that too.

Then. Today, I say amen to Harold's comments about my dad. In retrospect, I'm glad he was hard on me.

My oldest daughter thinks I'm hard on her. She wants everything her friends have. She wants to be able to go to the mall with her girlfriends whenever she wants. She wants to wear what she sees on television and she definitely thinks she has too much work to do around the house. I love my daughters. A part of me wants them to have all the things they want. The things I never had. I even want them to think of me as the cool father. But then I have to remind myself that I always thought my friends had cool parents. Kids having cool parents isn't the issue. Kids having real parents who believe in real parenting will determine how they live as adults.

Even though my parents raised me to see my peers as equals, they nonetheless made sure I understood what the rules were in our home. My mother in particular made no bones about the fact that my sisters and I were different than the other kids in our neighborhood. What other parents allowed or did not monitor had absolutely no effect on how they parented us.

Fortunately for me, my absolute number one, best friend, Cliff Johnson, lived directly across the alleyway from me and was being raised by his grandparents with rules very similar to my parents'. We often talked about how cool everybody else's parents were. Looking back with an adult, critical eye I realize now how important Cliff was to my development. He kept me from feeling alone.

One of the childhood lessons I took into my parenting role is that it is essential for kids not to be alone. They don't want to be alone. In fact they are afraid of being alone. They join gangs not to be alone. Girls have sex with guys they are not in love with so that they won't feel alone. And yet parents, teachers, ministers and other caring adults spend very little if any time helping kids learn how to pick the right crew to be with. My parents didn't teach me either, but they did limit my access to certain people. They didn't do it purposely. What happened is that because of my parents' restrictions on my activities, a lot of the kids in the neighborhood teased me. That limited my interest in hanging with them too much. On top of that, my parents' rules were such that a lot of things the other kids got to do, I couldn't go do. That limited my access to them. Cliff never teased me about my parents' rules. Why? Cliff and I were cool because he had the same basic restrictions. My other three friends that I mentioned earlier didn't tease Cliff or me very much, but they could go places and do things that we couldn't, so our access to them was also limited.

Thanks to the media today, we end up lumping all kids together. We talk about them in absolutes. "This generation...", "All you kids...", "Today's kids are...". The problem is that when we lump them all together, they tend to stay together. In other words when we put them together, they stick together. Groups develop their own culture. Unfortunately, sometimes the group's culture may not be conducive to learning. In some groups it isn't cool to be smart.

A couple of years ago my daughter Andrea made the honor roll at her school. I was happy and so was her mother. Andrea was upset. She was upset because she hadn't made the Principal's List. Honor roll means A's and B's. The Principal's List means all A's. I was glad she wasn't satisfied with honor roll, but the fact of the matter is that her dissatisfaction with honor roll had very little to do with the wonderful lectures she had heard from her mom and me about doing her best. It mainly had to do with the fact that her two best buddies at school both made Principal's List. She wanted to fit with her crew. That was a crew I liked her hanging with. Their culture was congruent with what her mother and I were trying to teach her. Unfortunately for us, those two young ladies no longer attend the same school as my daughter. My friend Cliff and I never attended the same school. He was a Catholic schoolboy while I was public school all the way. The good news for us was that we lived 40 seconds away from each other. My daughter's friends live quite a ways away.

One of the suggestions I have made to parents for years was to always know their child's two or three bestest, bestest friends—and their parents. Getting to know the friends will give you a chance to evaluate what their group norms might be regarding education, sex, drugs, dating and etc. At certain points in our children's development, their friends' approval is critical. Imagine what might have happened if my daughter's two best girlfriends thought getting on the honor roll or Principal's List was completely un-cool?

Listening to and observing my kids and their friends will give me a chance to better understand my child's world. This is crucial for a number of reasons. First and foremost, it is essential for your child's education. In learning situations, kids are pretty much like you and I. We best retain information that the brain considers relevant to our world. In today's America, your child's teacher may know very little about his or her world which means it's up to you to make sure your kids see the relevance. A few weeks ago I spoke in the beautiful village of Chisasibi in northern Quebec. Everyone was talking about one thing: the weather. It was the hottest day in recorded history for them: 42 degrees! Now, you're probably wondering how 42 could be the hottest day on record. Well, it probably slipped your mind that Canadians measure the temperature using the Celsius scale, while in America the Fahrenheit scale is used. Now, without consulting a book, calculator or the internet determine what the temperature is in Fahrenheit. Can't do it? I'm not surprised. Even though most of us learned about the relationship between Celsius and Fahrenheit and yet we did not retain it. Why? We didn't retain it because we didn't see the relevance to our world. Have you ever thought about the other things we teach kids in school today that your kids might not see the relevance or connection to the lives they're living day to day? Now, consider this, if it is clear to you that kids might not be able to see the connection to their world, are you sure that your child's teacher knows enough about your kid's world to help them make the connection?

Another critical issue we must help our kids with is the concept of delayed gratification. Unfortunately, as we have continued to give our kids all of the things that we never had, we have sold them on the reality of immediate gratification. As we discussed earlier, I am meeting more and more kids who tell me that they ultimately get everything they ask for. And they don't have to wait long for it. The result? They want what they want and they want it right now. Of course that leads to problems like poor credit in adulthood, but perhaps the biggest problem is that it hurts the educational process. Education is clearly a long-term investment. It is an example of long-term gratification. Look at it this way, if your kids never have to wait for and earn something, how do you teach them to wait for and work for educational attainment?

Stop giving your kids any and everything they want. Stop giving them all the things you didn't have. (Some of the things you didn't have, you didn't need.) We have to raise our kids in a way that mirrors life so that when they are on their own, life won't blow them away. In case you haven't figured it out yet, this is hard. The figuring out what to do isn't that hard. But it is very hard to watch your child flounder and make mistakes and feel embarrassed or frustrated in a situation. But it is an essential part of their development. Child psychologist and Tufts University Professor David Elkind puts it another way, "Kids need to feel badly sometimes. We learn through experience and we learn through bad experiences. Through failure we learn how to cope." What would have happened if the first time your child tried to stand up and then fell, you then stopped letting them try to stand on their own because you didn't want them to fall again? They would have eventually learned to stand and walk, but you would have severely retarded their growth. Thanks to their natural instincts—which I like to call the *baby code*—

they would have eventually learned because they would have kept trying when you were not around. Would any of us want our children to first have to learn to deal with failure when they are in college and get their first failing grade?

Have you ever taken the time to just watch babies? They are remarkable human beings. I found myself one Sunday afternoon sitting on the sofa in my den watching one of my daughters, Andrea, when she was about ten months old. She was trying to stand up on her own. Andrea must have attempted to stand up at least thirty times. Usually, she failed and tumbled back to her original position. But each time, she quickly regrouped and tried again. She never cried or threw a tantrum. In fact in many cases she broke out into laughter.

Have you ever watched a child go through this process? It is clear that they have a goal. They may not have words for it, but it is abundantly clear that they want to get up on two feet like everybody else and expand their world. They have no pre-conceived notions to limit them. No one has told them that they can't do it. No one has ever said to them that they are wasting their time. It never enters their mind that their goal cannot be reached. There is no clutter in their head.

If you watch the child long enough you will see them try to stand and fall. If they fall one way, the next time they will usually fall in the opposite direction. Why? It is because they are learning. They are testing their boundaries. They are learning what they can do. The most amazing thing about babies is that they actually come up with plans for reaching their goals.

Over and over again, my daughter would crawl to the end of the coffee table or the sofa and pull herself up to a standing position. As I said earlier, she'd fall, but then she'd go back to the edge of the sofa or the table and start over. No matter how often we picked her up, if we brought her back to the family room, she'd try to get to the edge of the sofa or table and try to pull up.

The more I watched Andrea, the more intrigued I became. Then a very important observation popped in my mind. Kids between the ages of one day and three years have an incredible success rate on reaching their major goals. You might try to explain this fact away by saying the infant's goals don't represent significant challenges. Well, let's consider that.

Two of the most obvious goals for kids at that age are to communicate with the people in their world and to stand up and walk on their own. In other words the child wants to: 1) master a language without a pre-existing language to use as a reference; and 2) control their bodies to the point that they can move around on their own. So, do you think that's easy? If you do, have a conversation with a physical therapist who has worked with an adult who has to re-learn how to walk, tie their shoes or bathe themselves. Ask those professionals how hard it is to re-teach adults those basic but very significant things.

Consider this: The only way babies can accomplish the incredible things that they do is because they keep trying. They fall down, but they get back up. Legendary college basketball coach John Wooden talked openly about the fact that he considered perseverance much more important in the scheme of things than pure talent or education. Adults often miss the mark on the successes we deserve, not because they are impossible for us, but simply because we don't persevere.

Conversely, babies seem to know that perseverance is critical to success. Since reaching that realization I started looking at some of the other secrets to winning. How many others did my daughter know at ten months old? Now you may be thinking, I never knew the secret to winning. Well I beg to differ. We all have been exposed to the secrets to winning. Some of us just forgot.

Let's talk further about how babies do the incredible things they do. Recall a time when you observed a baby in a crib, or while holding it. The next time you do keep in mind the book, *How Babies Think: The Science of Childhood.* The book points out that when we look at babies, we see their innocence and helplessness. But the truth is, that baby is the most powerful learning machine in the universe.

Success. By definition it is the attainment of a goal or objective. One of the beautiful things about life is that every living soul has experienced success. Its concept and the feeling of success are not foreign to any of us. From learning to feed ourselves or tie our shoes as children, we all have a track record of success. The other side of that coin is that each of us has even more experience with failure. In fact, we typically have to go through failure to reach success.

The toddler learning to walk will undoubtedly fall down hundreds of times before mastering the process. Similarly a rookie quarterback, drafted number one in the NFL will make dozens if not hundreds of mistakes in practice and in games before mastering the pro game. Professional baseball's two most prolific and successful homerun hitters of all time, Hank Aaron and Babe Ruth, were also two of the most common strike out victims. Wait a minute. I don't think you heard me.

Hank Aaron and Babe Ruth had more failures than successes. Hammerin' Hank Aaron had 1,383 career strikeouts to accompany his magnanimous 755 homeruns in his career to go along with his. George Herman (Babe) Ruth smashed 714 homers and whiffed 1,330 times. In other words, failure is the rite of passage to success. We all have our own personal history of success and failure unless our parents protected and shielded us from failure. What might have happened if either Hank Aaron's parents or Babe Ruth's folks were of today's era and had stopped taking them to little league baseball because they struck out their first twenty times at the plate?

Another critical element in a baby's success formula is a cheering section. Babies will cause the most serious and intense of adults to act like blithering idiots. When my daughter was trying to walk, every time she tried to get up and walk, I was in the background cheering her on. "That's it, you can do it! That's Daddy's big girl."

And when she'd fall I'd say, "Oopsy daisy." She'd get right back up and I'd be there cheering her on again. I wasn't the only cheerleader in the bleachers. Her mother, grandparents, aunts, uncles and friends of the family were cheering right along with me. With all that support and encouragement babies never give up on their goals. They keep going for it. I am convinced that now that my Andrea is 13 going on 30, my role is still similar. I watch her spread her wings and try more things. I cheer her on, but I allow her to fall down. I encourage her to get up, but I allow her to fail and then try again.

Believe it or not I learned that from my dad, a career postal employee with only two years of college. Today we find that the fastest increases in depression and anxiety rates are among children. Harvard psychologist Jerome Kagan's research on children's temperaments has determined that what creates anxious children is parents hovering and protecting them from stressful experiences.

One of the things I have found speaking to so many different kinds of people is that we are more alike than we are unique. We all have fears, doubts and insecurities. We've all had victories and defeats. Yet, we tend to fall into one of two categories. One group is full of people who are so afraid of failing and spend so much time looking at the possibility of failure, that they disregard or discount their successes waiting around for the failure they expect.

The good news is that there's a second, smaller group who still act like babies. They seem to have a winner's aura. They focus more on their pattern of success and expect to win. They fall down, but they get up. Have you ever noticed the determination kids have when there is something they have decided they want to do?

Could you imagine having a workforce with that same kind of commitment to a task? Maybe that's what my old coach meant when he talked about being pure in heart. Who could be more pure in heart than an infant?

As I said before, this ain't rocket science. If the problem is that we buy kids too much and it skews their concept of money, then cut the money. A good way to teach them about money is to put them in charge of some of the money you have allotted for them. If you have figured out that you need maybe twenty dollars a week for your elementary school kid to cover bus fare, lunch, snacks, church offering, etc. Give it to them with a list of what they have to cover. Teach them how to keep a log of every penny they spend which they need to go over with you at the end of the week. If they run out of money before handling everything then let them do without if the item isn't a necessity. This is a wonderful way to give kids a safe place to begin to understand that in this world if you misman-age your funds, you will have to do without certain things. In the jungle if the young animal does not learn to hunt or forage it will eventually die.

If your kid is the type who doesn't like to work, try setting up a work schedule for him or her at an early age. Hold them accountable for the work they have to do. When my youngest was four, my wife started putting a weekly chore assignment sheet on the refrigerator door for both of the girls. She also put one on each of their beds. They both understood at that tender age that they were responsible for handling their lists. They also understood that if they did not handle their lists, there would be consequences. The scary thing is that a few times I read my little one's chore list to some kids at a high school. Quite a few of them chuckled and claimed that my then five-year old had more work to do around the house than they did. What would your child have said?

•

Are You Ready
for Some
Football?

A few years ago the Fellowship of Christian Athletes invited me to deliver a speech to over 2,000 kids in San Diego the day before the Super Bowl. That night I got a phone call in my hotel room from the Broncos' chaplain. The Broncos' defensive captain, Neil Smith had suggested they invite me to speak at their chapel service before they left the hotel for the game. I was thrilled! It was an old college ball player's dream. To top it off, Grammy award-winning gospel singer CeCe Winans was there to sing before and after I spoke.

The Broncos were serious underdogs that year and very few football aficionados gave them much chance to beat the reigning Super Bowl Champions, the Green Bay Packers.

The night before, I agonized about what to say to a group of world-class athletes who had reached the pinnacle of their craft. A group of athletes who Coach Moore would say were pure in heart. Then, at last it hit me. I decided to talk about the fact that simply wanting to win was not enough. Just like simply wanting to make the pro's when they were in college was not enough. For those who came to pre-season camp overweight, simply wanting to lose weight was not enough. Wanting a good marriage is never enough. Wanting well-disciplined, independent kids is not enough.

They had to build on their history of success. Revisit the things they had committed to in the past that helped them succeed. My daddy used to say the same thing to my sisters another way: When you go to the dance, you dance wit' who brung you.

I wanted to make sure they remembered the formula for winning that had brought them to the biggest dance of their professional lives. Some of us have found success on the job or in our personal or family lives and have never given conscious thought to what got us there. We will tell people that it just sort of happened and that may be true, but I doubt it. Very few worthwhile things just sort of happen. Besides what is the message for our kids if we let them believe that good things just sort of happen? In a study published in the August 2004 issue of *Personality and Social Psychology Review* children and college students of today believe that their futures are out of their control, much more so than children and college students in the 1960s and 1970s. Psychology professor Jean Twenge from the University of San Diego put it this way in the *Atlanta Journal-Constitution*, "If you believe success comes from luck rather than hard work, why work hard?" What do your kids think? How does that help our kids buy into the long-term nature of education? If you are a manager or an entrepreneur, what do your employees think?

Remember, there is no special advantage or magic and the playing field is pretty level or as Thomas Friedman asserts in his new book, the playing field is now pretty flat. So, our wins don't just happen. I am convinced that whether we are consciously aware of them or not, our adherence to the baby code is where the rubber meets the road.

With the underdog Broncos (who had already lost four previous Super Bowl appearances) I started by comparing the Super Bowl to the biblical showdown between the underdog of all time, David and the arrogantly under whelmed Goliath. Did David want to win? Absolutely. This was a fight to the finish. If he didn't win, his people would be enslaved and he would die.

For the same reasons, Goliath also wanted to win. I asked the Broncos if they wanted to win. In typical football style they roared back a deafening "Yes!" I then reminded them that the Packers would say the same thing. In other words, the wanting had to be transformed into positive action.

The good news, as I told them, was that most of the work had already been done:

1) They had a shared, visible, believable goal. In other words, they all knew what they wanted: A Super Bowl Championship. Key: Shared Vision.

2) They had individually and collectively been preparing for this game for months, even years. In the weight room. On the practice field. Looking at film after film after film. Studying the playbook. They knew their personal strengths and weaknesses and had learned over time to lean on the strengths and compensate for the weaknesses. Key: Preparation.

3) The general manager and coaching staff had put together the right raw materials. They had studied their opponent's strengths and weaknesses and had designed a solid game plan. Key: Developed game plan.

4) They had practiced, practiced and practiced some more. They had fallen down, jumped off sides and made mistakes together. They had broken bread together, laughed together, fought each other and cried together. They liked each other. It was all about building a team.
Key: Proper Preparation.

Now it was simply time to approach this game with the confidence that says "I know we can do this. Not only can we win this game, but we will!" It was time to GO for it!

Compare the Broncos to the average baby learning to walk.

1. Both the Broncos and the babies had very clear goals. The Broncos to win the Lombardi Trophy and the babies to become bipeds. (To walk on two feet like everyone else.)

2. The Broncos' coaches knew well the strengths and weaknesses of their players because they had been gauging them since training camp, while the babies constantly test their limits trying to discover their strengths and weaknesses.

3. Just like my daughter had a plan to help her get to her feet, the Broncos had an extensive game plan.

4. Similar to the cheerleading section that my daughter had in her corner, the Bronco's had over half the stadium pulling for them.

5. The one advantage a baby has over the Super Bowl participants is that their minds have not been encumbered. No one has ever told the baby that they can't do it. From the minute they'd won the AFC Title game, every media outlet in the country went on and on about how the Broncos had lost all four of their previous tries.

Is it just me, or does it strike you as a little weird that babies do naturally what we have to remind adults to do? It's not so strange when you realize that babies are simply using tools that each of us is born with, but too often parents intervene and force kids away from the code for so long that they lose touch with it.

Earlier this year I went to my family's biennial reunion in Meridian, Mississippi. Meridian is the closest town of any size to our family's actual hometown, Shubuta, Mississippi. My daughters were a little amazed to find that we had family there from all over. The New York contingent was there, the Chicago crew came on Amtrak, the Los Angeles and Texas clan came together. For some reason we have quite a few attorneys in my family. At one point I looked at one table and it was pretty much full of attorneys and on the other side of the room was a table full of people who often needed attorneys. In other words, my family is very diverse. During the banquet my dad's oldest living sister shared with us some of the family history. She started during the latter days of slavery and brought us to the present. I found myself getting choked up when she talked about her father, my grandfather E.G. Creagh.

My grandfather and his father were amazing men. When he died, my grandfather had accumulated over 400 acres of land in the heart of Mississippi. Some of my older cousins remember the Ku Klux Klan burning crosses in front of my grandfather's home. People used to call my grandfather Professor Creagh even though he didn't have his doctorate. It was simply a sign of respect for his leadership in the community.

He helped build the local church and school. He also taught at the school. My grandfather even owned land in the town of Waynesboro, Mississippi, which was almost of unheard of at that time. As you think about the things that E.G. Creagh accomplished, keep in mind that he did this during the middle of the Jim Crow era. In other words, he wasn't supposed to be able to pull this off. Not in Mississippi! But he did.

Now fast forward to the present day. One of the things that hit me while sitting at my family reunion was how I had so many cousins and nieces and nephews who were raised with so many more opportunities than my grandfather and his siblings and yet almost to the man and woman, they all accomplished more. Much more. Why? I think the answer to the question is simple. They accomplished more because they knew they had to. Being born into a time when slavery was more than just a history lesson to their parents and grandparents they knew how bad bad could be. Likewise, their children knew it as well. No matter how much they may have wanted to, survival demanded that they not shield their kids from the truth of the world around them. In essence, they had to grow up young. One immature act or irresponsible act at the wrong time could mean the difference between life and death, survival and demise.

My grandparents and their peers also knew they had previously unprecedented opportunities, even though their parents had no assets to give them other than a passion and determination to be successful, a commitment to hard work and a thirst for education. With that, they changed the lives and lot of our entire family. Unfortunately, many of my uncles and aunts did not pass those assets on to their children. The end result is that even fewer of those assets are being passed on to the grandkids.

Now, don't misunderstand. Not all African origin people of my grandfather's era accomplished as much as he did. Unfortunately, that is not the way a capitalist environment works. My grandfather's peers did have the same level of opportunities and obstacles however. The question is what the individual does with the opportunities and obstacles they face.

While writing this book I got a phone call from one of my old collegiate friends. He and I pledged our fraternity together back in our late teens. I don't think we've seen each other more than just in passing in nearly twenty years. But in college we were pretty good friends. He called recently because he just needed to vent. Staring at his upcoming fiftieth birthday, he had been thinking about his life and felt as though maybe he had wasted a lot of it. He felt that many of our friends had outdone him career wise and financially. My frat brother majored in education and is an excellent teacher, yet he looks at many of his friends and associates in other fields who make more money than he does and gets angry. He looks at his friends in education who are in higher status level and paying administrative jobs and he gets mad. He's not angry at his friends and associates, he's angry at himself.

The truth of the matter is that my buddy could have done a lot more in education or a number of other fields. We all had the same level of opportunities and obstacles. The question is what the individual does with the opportunities and obstacles they face. In college quite a few of my fraternity brothers used to tease me because they said I was too serious about school. I wasn't the only one that got teased. There were about five of us who weren't the party animals or girl chasers that some of them were. We were the geeks.

Conversely, we thought they were irresponsible and undependable when it came to handling business. Surprisingly, when I talked to my old friend the brothers he was comparing himself to were not those in the geek category back in the day. It's almost as though he didn't expect to do as well as we geeks. He was upset because he felt he hadn't done as well as some of the party animals. During our conversation I had to admit to him that in college I was always envious of how so many girls were crazy about him.

In college, he always had the prettiest girls. But looking back, I must acknowledge that we all had the same level of opportunities and obstacles when it came to the opposite sex. The question is always what the individual does with the opportunities and obstacles they face.

In short, my fraternity brother was beginning to have a midlife crisis. A midlife crisis basically means we take stock of where we are in our lives in comparison to where we thought we'd be. My buddy's exploration could cause him to change careers at an inopportune time. One of my good friends did that a few years ago. He decided his wonderful wife wasn't enough of a hottie, so he divorced her and moved a girl in who was younger than all of his daughters. Little does he know how many of his old buddies chuckle and crack jokes about his decision making behind his back. The point is simply this, folks: we are all presented with opportunities. How your kids take advantage of those opportunities is where the rubber meets the road.

When my children leave my house they need those four character traits ingrained in them that I mentioned before: responsibility, accountability, dependability, and maturity.

Think about it for a minute. If you owned a business how many immature, irresponsible, undependable employees who refuse to be held accountable for their actions would you want on your payroll? More significantly, how many could you afford to have on your payroll and for how long could you carry them? In addition to these character traits, my girls must have a commitment to hard work, a thirst for education, and it is critical that they understand that thing called relationship as well.

Successful parenting is not about making a baby. It is about raising an adult. It is our most important job. It is also an increasingly difficult job. America has changed significantly and is still in the process of tremendous change. My children must grow up with more than a basic education and they must have work ethic or very simply they will not survive the future in today's America. Yours either.

When I was a kid I remember visiting cousins and aunts and uncles who barely had high school educations, but they lived incredibly well. One of the great things about the old America was that our middle class was so strong that a person could have a high school diploma and as long as they could get in the local union and were willing to work hard and work some overtime, they could make great money. Their jobs were hard and often tedious, but they required either low or moderate skill levels. As a result, it wasn't essential for kids to do great in high school. Today however, thanks to technology and outsourcing things are different. Many jobs have been eliminated because computers can do them and the computer doesn't want a lunch break or need health insurance. In many other cases, technology has allowed the grunt work of a company that was often done by the lowest on the totem pole to be shipped over seas. If you call an American airline today, their reservation lines are most likely going to be answered by young people in Bangalore, India who can't even afford to ride on an American airliner. There are currently 245,000 Indians in Bangalore working in call centers for companies from all over the globe. They are answering customer service calls, taking credit card orders, making hotel reservations, selling goods and services, trouble-shooting computer problems and on and on and on.

In 2003, American firms outsourced the completion of 25,000 U.S. tax returns to India. In 2004 the number was 100,000. In 2005, the number is expected to be 400,000! The IRS has even outsourced a lot of their work processing those same returns.

The message is clear. A lot of companies that used to hire kids when they were teens and young adults now simply are not interested in them anymore. Add to that the fact that many of the companies that hired low to moderate skill level adults aren't interested in our young adults and clearly we have a national problem.

Just Say
NO!

~~~~~~~~~~

It has been a number of years now that I have been discussing these phenomena and after almost every session, I meet parents who come up to me and say that I have just described their home. Their next question is always, "How do I fix it?" That question is quickly followed by, "My kid is already a teen. Is it too late to turn it around?" Well, the good news is that it is never too late to start. The first thing most of us need to do is go stand in front of a mirror and practice saying one word: "No!"

Now, don't misunderstand, I'm not talking about saying no to your child every time they ask for something *else*. You have to start by saying NO to yourself. Say no to that part of you that has associated giving children what they want with showing how much you love them. If you think about it, part of showing love is teaching boundaries and restraint. Unfortunately, a lot of us act like restraint is synonymous with mistreatment. Mom! Dad! They are two different things! Let's think that through. If we give our kids everything they want, then that means we love them. If we insist on moderate restraint and boundaries then we are mistreating them. Back up mom and dad. Read that again. Giving apparently equals love and restraint and boundaries equal mistreatment. Give me a break.

I just returned from giving a talk to a parent group based on this manuscript. One mom said she hopes her teenaged son can take care of himself. She already has one of her other children living with them—in a dependent state. Her *45* year-old daughter! Wow!

A father at a corporate session pulled me aside during a break and asked if I could come home with him and have a discussion with his family. He always tried to make his kids work and he would not buy them everything. Unfortunately, his wife would go behind his back and tell them they didn't have to finish whatever chore he had assigned them. She also bought them things he had told them they could not have. Today, he and his wife have four twenty-something kids living at home and not paying rent or utilities beyond their cell phone. I gave the brother a hug.

Everywhere I go, parents can relate. While in Bermuda recently one mother talked about a young woman at her job, maybe nineteen or twenty who was terminated because she had a nasty habit of laying her head down on her desk and taking a nap after lunch. At the same session I heard from a father who is an entrepreneur. He told us about a good friend whose fifteen-year old son has approximately $3000 worth of sneakers.

Maybe your kids don't need it, but my children need to understand restraint and boundaries. When they finally leave my home —and leave they will—I want them to understand that you can't go hang out all night and be your sharpest during the day at work. In other words you can't burn the candle on both ends and still expect to find success. I want my daughters to understand that young ladies and young men need to have boundaries that are based on what is appropriate for the environment they wish to live in.

Recently while doing a session for a client in Alabama, I was amazed at the reaction the class had to my story about the young men who lost their jobs for repeated use of the "n" word. Almost every manager in the room had a similar story. One told of a black female employee he has been trying to talk to about use of the "n" word. Another told of a black male employee whom they wanted to promote, but they really wanted him to try coming to work without his customary doo rag. Unfortunately, the young man in question thought that might be giving up too much of his cultural identity. Amazing? Again, I beg you to give me a break! Again, I have to ask, *What in the world is going on?*

About the same time I heard a manager from another client complain that he had a young African American employee who wouldn't take off his bandana. His boss was concerned about whether it might indicate gang affiliation. You and I might question the fairness or even the legality of his concern. I am not here to discuss the politics. My point is that regardless of whether or not his boss ever brought up his concerns, that young employee was always going to be viewed by his supervisor through the lens of doubt and trepidation. You tell me, do you think this kid is ever going to be recommended for a promotion by his boss?

Maybe you think I'm getting paranoid in my old age or that I am bashing young people but please don't misunderstand who or what I am. My vocation and avocation alike is to help kids make better decisions. Primarily over the years I have focused on impacting their thoughts and decisions about illegal drug and alcohol usage. I have taken four different young people into my home for varying amounts of time. The point is that I LOVE OUR KIDS!

I love our kids and right now I am petrified about what I am seeing around America. Just a while back I went to my favorite IHOP. Before I said a word the hostess immediately seated me in the section covered by my favorite waitress, Del. Del is Indian and approximately

114

40 to 45 years old. (Guess why she's my favorite?) Seated near me was a group of managers from a local rent-to-own company. It was pretty clear who the boss was, since he did all of the talking and some of the others looked very nervous. I couldn't help but pick up part of their conversation. A couple of comments made me stick around after I had finished my breakfast. I waited until most of the troops had left and then introduced myself to the boss. I told him a little about my book and asked him what his experience had been with younger employees. He chuckled a humorless chuckle and asked me how much time I had because that could take all day.

His first words were, "They don't have work ethic." He went on to explain that quite a few of the young folks he had hired felt the jobs they were qualified for were beneath them. They weren't willing to do the types of jobs that he began his career with. It's as though they want the job that he worked up to over a ten-year career with the company on day one. But they don't want to put in the work to get there.

He also said that many of them just would not dress right for the job. Sagging pants and an overall sloppy look for the guys and too much skintight clothing and exposed skin on the young ladies. Excessive jewelry, tattoos, piercings and grills for both sexes.

That conversation motivated me to look around the restaurant to see how many young people were working there. The youngest waitress was one I avoided like the plague. She is African American and maybe 25 years old. One day my normal server (Del) was off and they seated me in this young lady's section. She came over to see if I would like a cup of coffee to get started. I had wanted coffee until she smiled and I saw the full gold grill she had over her teeth. Strike one! Then when she brought me some additional silverware later she carried it in her hand by the part that would go in my mouth. Strike two! Finally, at one point during my meal, she referred to me as "dog." Now, I know dog is an accepted term in today's society and I have friends who sometimes call me dog, but I really don't want the waiters at the IHOP calling me that. Strike three!

When Del came to bring my check I asked her about the lack of young people on the wait staff and she told me that the owners tried very hard to hire young people, but it was a problem. She said most of them only stayed somewhere between three and four weeks— just long enough for them to be trained. She said most of them just didn't want to work. (Her words—not mine.) They routinely came late and often called in at the last minute and didn't come at all. I also found out that many of the older more mature and responsible workers didn't like working with them because customers in the young people's sections would start asking them for assistance because the young workers were moving too slow or forgetting them. She finally said the only young people who lasted were Mexican immigrants and Asians. White kids and black kids just didn't want to work.

One of the benefits of my career is that I get to travel throughout this great country of ours and the bad news is that I am seeing this phenomenon everywhere. In Mechanicsburg, Pennsylvania I had a chance to chat with a group of managers from a company that an entrepreneur built from a $17,000 investment to over $70 million in annual sales. One of the managers shared with me that almost 75% of their terminations were tied to attendance and punctuality. One particular employee had continually returned late from lunch during the first two weeks of his employment. They told him in no uncertain terms that his behavior was unacceptable and would not be tolerated. Finally, they terminated him. The amazing thing was when they fired him he was shocked. Again, I keep getting evidence that leads me to believe that for quite a few of our young people the first time someone tells them that certain behavior is unacceptable and will not be tolerated and they absolutely mean it, is when they get into the workplace.

Recently while in the metro Chicago area I met with a group of student leaders at Lincoln Way Central High School. One of the young people shared with me that over the summer she worked at a local Baskin Robbins owned by an Asian Indian family. She said the Indian family often comment and joke about the lack of work ethic they saw in American youngsters. She said the owners seemed to work nonstop. Interestingly, the seventeen-year old white female said she agreed with her former employer's assessment.

I spoke at a deep suburban middle school earlier this week. (A deep suburban school is one located in an area that has recently been labeled a suburb of a major city even though just a few or two years ago, it was considered the country.) I was talking to over 500 sixth graders. Two young girls—maybe 12 years old, one white and one black—were sitting in the front row and their blouses were open so far down their chest, I was embarrassed for them. There was a young man at the program who came in wearing all blue oversized clothing. It was made of some type of khaki or canvas material. I asked the kid what he was wearing. He kinda' tried to not to slip off the slippery slope and asked me one thing. "What do you mean?" I tried another approach. "What's up with your outfit?" Again, he replied "What?" Then out of the bleachers came a voice: "That's gang stuff." The kids knew! But did the faculty? Here's bottom line question: Why didn't a parent question their attire before they left the house?

I had a very interesting experience at my local bank. First, understand that the branch I use is located in a grocery store. As usual, the teller line was very long and I was currently at the end of said line. A young black woman, approximately 22 or 23 years old, was directly in front of me. She was having an animated conversation with a young man accompanying her. They were talking loud enough that I heard their entire conversation. Unfortunately, almost everyone else in line did also. The young woman was going on and on about one of the tellers. She felt he was a slow worker and obviously he really bothered her. She talked about an earlier experience she'd had with the teller where he apparently recounted some cash she was depositing more than a couple of times. Her obvious insinuation was that he was not very bright. I have worked with the same teller before and he is very deliberate at times. It is also clear that he is either mentally or physically challenged. Beyond that, the only comment I can make is that he is one of my two preferred tellers.

What really struck me about their conversation—other than their rudeness—was that the young lady eventually mentioned that she needed to get a pre-paid cell phone. Her cell phone had been disconnected by Cingular because of an unpaid bill of $500. When her friend questioned her about the amount she explained that she had been out of work for over six months. She said if she wasn't getting paid, Cingular wasn't getting paid. When he asked why she left her job, she said she quit because they were on her nerves. I'm sorry folks, I must be getting old, because the way I was raised you don't just up and quit a job without having another lined up because they were on your nerves. But that's only part of the story. She went on to say that she was supposed to be at work, but when she woke up that morning she didn't feel like being bothered. So, she called in sick. What do you think her friend's response was? He grinned and said, "I know that's right."

Now for those of you who don't know, "I know that's right" in this situation is an affirmation that her thinking and logic are sound. THEY ARE NOT! How much would you wager that the teller she didn't want to be bothered with would absolutely never treat his employer like that? I wanted to yell out at her that if I needed to hire someone and she and the teller were my two choices, he'd get the job hands down. Instead, I just shook my head.

So, let's recap, the problem exists in the fast food industry, grocery industry, automobile manufacturing, insurance, restaurant and retail. Oh, I forgot an industry: education. I have heard from a number of school administrators that they are seeing some of the same lack of commitment and work ethic in some of their younger teachers. I have seen it throughout the U. S., but not just in the United States. Okay, so where does all of this information leave us?

The truth of the matter is that when I started seeing what was happening to our kids I got seriously depressed. Not just because of what was transpiring, but more because I had to admit that I had not been doing everything I could to help ensure that my kids would be ready for the world. To say the least, it is very humbling to know that under the banner of love I may have been preparing my children for a life of irrelevance.

Irrelevance. By definition, irrelevant means to not be relevant. Relevant is to have bearing on the matter at hand. If the matter at hand that we are dealing with is the workforce, we live in a highly competitive environment called the United States of America—actually, we live in a highly competitive environment called the *world*.

Getting Fired Up About the Future

Earlier this week I went to get a haircut. I go to a typical, old-fashioned black barbershop. In the midst of all of the pseudo intellectual conversations going on covering everything from a former Atlanta mayor's indiscretions to the NBA All-Star game, my barber, who may be 28, asked one of his colleagues a question. He wanted to know if the younger barber had been the kind of kid who got straight A's in school. The other barber answered without any humor, sarcasm or real emotion, "No. I didn't get smart till later. I had too many distractions in school."

Think about what he said. When he was a kid he didn't understand the importance or significance of the things he was going to need to be successful. Like your kids and mine, he wanted to do what he wanted to do. It reminds me of some of the things I have heard from guys who have spent time in prison and started reading and learning. Many have gone on to get degrees. Many have found that they really like learning. Do you think they might be able to borrow the answer I heard in the barbershop? *I didn't get smart till later. I had too many distractions.*

It made me wonder why I got smart earlier than they did. Was it something innate inside me? Is it heredity or environment? For me, I'd have to say environment. Why? Because it was my momma and daddy's environment I lived in, which meant it wasn't completely up to me what I did with my time. My momma and daddy thought a major part of their job was keeping me from getting distracted. In other words, I didn't get smart any sooner than they did. In my parents' home, I didn't have to get smart early. They were smart for me and based on that smartness, there were certain things that I absolutely had to do and other things that I absolutely could not do. Did I always agree with their decisions? Definitely not. Yet if we make decisions for our kids based solely on whether they will agree or like those decisions are we really doing what is best for our kids? I don't think so.

Please don't conclude from anything I have shared that there is a big national or global conspiracy to hurt our kids. Quite to the contrary, I think there is national concern for our kids. This situation is no more than a continuation of what has been going on in America for generations. My parents wanted my sisters and me to do better than they did. They wanted to give us a lot of the things that they never had—and they did. Your parents were probably the same.

Unfortunately, in many cases we aren't giving our kids some of the things they need the most. You see, the latest sneakers aren't critical to their futures. Neither are the latest designer bags or shoes or newest video games or mp3's. I am convinced that there are certain critical things that your child must leave your house with in order to be successful. Kids must leave the nest FIRED UP! Or better yet:

F

I

R

E

D

U

P

!

As we discussed earlier, more and more of our young people are finding themselves in serious financial trouble often before they even finish college. Many end up back at home because they just can't afford to make it on their own. With that in mind, I think it is critical that our kids leave home with more than just our blessings. They must leave with FINANCIAL SAVVY. They really must begin to understand money. Earlier I mentioned having your kids keep track of how they spend their money, but since that time I have been learned of a young mother in the Los Angeles area who has come up with a wonderful vehicle to teach very young kids about money. Her name is Lori Mackey. Lori wrote a wonderful book for primary grade kids called *Money Mama and the Three Little Pigs.* If you really want to help turn around your kids financially, then check out Lori's website at www.prosperity4kids.com. Keep in mind that Lori's material is designed for little ones but it can be adjusted for older kids. I also hear that she is in the process of putting together a program for older kids as well. Keep checking that website. One of the ideas that I borrowed from Lori for my kids is working incredibly well. Lori recommends that parents figure out just how much money you will have to spend on your kids monthly for school lunches, transportation, movies, cell phone bills, etc. Then brain storm and write down every item of work your child needs to do daily and weekly. Once that is done, put a dollar value on each item. At the end of the week I give my daughters a paycheck based on the items they complete. Once they get their check, they have to put a minimum of 20% into a savings account and 10% must be donated to charity. A key tie in is that once I start paying them, **I do not pay for anything else for them.** If they want to go to a movie, they must pay their own way. If they want to buy a soda at the convenience store, they must pay for it. Another key tie in is that if they don't do their chores, then of course they don't get paid. Additionally, if I do one of their chores for them, then they must pay me. For example, if my youngest daughter is supposed to clean the bathrooms on one side of the house and the dollar value for that chore is $5.00, but she doesn't do it—if I do it while she is at school—then when she gets her check, she must pay me the $5.00. The lesson I want them to get is that if you have something to do and you don't do it, there is a cost.

If your kids are in high school, consider buying them Suze Orman's book, *The Money Book for the Young, Fabulous and Broke*. Also consider letting your kids help you pay the bills sometime. It's okay to let them know that it is tough for you to make ends meet.

FINANCIAL SAVVY
I
R
E
D

U
P
!

The next thing I am convinced our kids need is INTELLECTUAL CAPITAL. Increasingly, the better jobs require more technical knowledge and in today's market the only real job security is your skill level and abilities. Hence, it is no longer a nice buzzword to talk about the concept of lifelong learning. Now it is an essential part of your plan for success. Constantly, your child needs to be adding to their intellectual bank account.

Again, keep in mind, the issue is not that there will be no jobs available. Quite to the contrary, with Baby Boomers hitting their 60's we are about to see the beginning of a mass exodus from the workforce. Some estimates are that over the next ten years almost 40% of the fulltime workforce will hit traditional retirement age. The February 18th, 2006 issue of *The Economist* highlighted the shortage of expertise looming for many industries. They highlighted the aerospace and defense industry as one that will see in many companies as much as 40% of their workforce becoming eligible for retirement in the next five years. Add to that fact, the reality that the number of engineering graduates in developed countries is in steep decline.

Lack of jobs is not the problem! Our kids not being prepared skill-wise for the better jobs is one problem. A second problem is that a lot of our kids who have not gotten themselves prepared for the better jobs, honestly feel that the lower skill level jobs are beneath them. Hence, we hear comments from people like Mexican President Vicente Fox that a lot of immigrants are simply coming into the U. S. A. to take the jobs that Americans don't want. We might not like hearing President Fox's comments but the truth in his words is undeniable. It amazed me when American's had a knee jerk reaction to those comments even though our own president, George W. Bush has made similar comments. Whenever the discussion of immigration reform has come up, President Bush has often commented about Mexican immigrants working jobs that Americans don't want. Our kids have to learn that you can't have it both ways. It is either one or the other. If you don't want the bottom level, labor-intensive jobs, then you must increase your intellectual capital to be able to compete for the better jobs. If you don't want to increase your intellectual capital, then you must be willing to accept the more labor intensive, low skill level jobs.

Because of the current shortage of low skilled American labor and impending shortage of skilled labor, corporations have had to begin to explore their options. One of those options has been to find ways to import skilled labor into the country. Another has been by trying to export certain jobs out of the country into parts of the world where there are eager potential workers. A third option has been to find ways to encourage seniors to either remain in the workplace longer or return if they have already left. With that in mind a lot of companies are exploring the ergonomics of their facilities to make jobs less strength dependent and less tiring.

What that all amounts to is that in the near future our kids will not only compete with their peer group. They must also compete with foreign students, immigrants, foreign-based labor forces and boomers who are delaying full retirement. As a parent, I feel that I must make sure that my kids understand where their competition is coming from and that just like in sports, they cannot take any competitor lightly.

FINANCIAL SAVVY
INTELLECTUAL CAPITAL
R
E
D

U
P
!

I have always felt that one of the problems kids are faced with comes directly from Mom and Dad. So many parents have told their kids that they can do anything, that they actually believe it. Everybody cannot become the next Bill Gates or Michael Jordan or Michelle Wie or Tiger Woods or George W. Bush or even Ozzie Osbourne. They also tend to think that they can do anything and have everything with little or no effort. You and I know that this could not be further from the truth. My kids must be ready to face the world with a REALISTIC PERSPECTIVE of themselves and life.

In a recent conversation a regional manager of a retail company said that many of his young employees thought the entry level positions were beneath them. They wanted to be where he and his managers were. The regional manager's comment to me was, "They don't understand that their store managers and I all started in the same position they're in. We had to work our way up." In other words, their skill set and experience level did not match where they thought they should be. Believe it or not, that is not abnormal. What is abnormal is that unlike past generations who understood they had to pay their dues before the good jobs and opportunities came their way, this generation is so used to immediate gratification that they don't think they should have to wait. Add to that the fact that they have grown up in a world where we have resisted ever giving them information that makes them feel bad and they aren't hearing what the corporations are saying.

It is important to accept the fact that we first started messing up our kids' perspective a whole lot earlier. One day I watched a mother and her toddler at a local retail store. The child was throwing quite a tantrum because of a toy she wanted. After trying to quiet the youngster, the mom finally reached over and grabbed the toy and handed it to her daughter in the shopping cart with the admonition for her to now keep quiet. She did. Later when I was leaving the store, I saw them again. The little girl was screaming at the top of her lungs—again. This time she wanted some kind of cookie. Mom gave it to her. It looked like blackmail to me. More importantly, what are we teaching kids when we allow this kind of behavior? Maybe, that bad behavior pays? How realistic is that?

Not sure? Ask a teacher. I already have. In fact, I have asked a number of teachers in every state and country I have visited lately. When I described the above scenario to them, I then asked them if that child's behavior—and more importantly, the mother's response to it—could have any impact on that child's success in the classroom. To put it another way, I wanted to know how would it impact their ability if they did not have to work at home. Guess what they said?

We cannot continue to bribe kids. It is a bastardization of the If-Then theory. In its pure form it goes like this: *If you finish all of your homework, then you can watch tv before going to bed.* Instead in the cases above we are saying, *If you scream, then I'll get you a new toy. If you pout, then I'll let you do whatever you want. If you don't do your chores, then I will do them for you and if you labor deeply over your homework, I'll do it for you.* If we send this message repeatedly, we end up raising a generation of young people whose perspective on what the realities of life and the workplace are, is extremely skewed.

Talking to a group of students who stuck around after a session I did at a high school in Ohio recently, I started asking each of them what they wanted to do in the future. Quite a few of them mentioned stuff like, doctor, engineer, computer technician, lawyer and accountant—which sounded good. Then I asked them what their grades were like. About two-thirds of them admitted that their grades were sub-par. I also asked them if they felt they could have done better in school if they had pushed themselves more. One hundred percent of them said yes. I really believe it is critical for parents, teachers, coaches and other adults to help young people look at their lives more realistically. If they really want to pursue their dreams then they must be willing to push themselves much harder. If they aren't willing to work harder, they might need to lower their goals.

FINANCIAL SAVVY
INTELLECTUAL CAPITAL
REALISTIC PERSPECTIVE
E
D

U
P
!

The revised and updated *Illustrated Oxford Dictionary* defines ethics as a set of moral principles. It further defines ethical as being morally correct and honorable. We live in a society of people and as such, in order to co-exist one with the other it is imperative that we operate in an ethical fashion. Believe it or not, ethical behavior is not something kids just pick up on their own. It is taught. For our purposes I want to concentrate on an ETHICAL APPROACH TO WORK. Loosely stated, it means we must approach our jobs in a morally correct and honorable way. So what does that really mean? To me it means what my daddy used to say: *Give a man an honest day's work for an honest dollar.* If you agree to work for someone, then you give that person your all.

That seems like good old common sense, but at some point when you talk about kids, it has to be taught to them. Notice, I quoted earlier what my daddy used to say. He taught it to me. But not just through lecture. More than anything else he taught it by example. So did my mother. They both worked. Every day for years I watched them get up and get ready for work. Every day they actually went to work and they got there on time. Perhaps most significantly, when I heard them talk about their jobs, every other word was not negative. I knew there were a couple of people at my mother's job that she didn't like very much—mainly because she thought they were not pulling their share of the weight. She didn't like their work ethic.

Like most things adults have internalized by the time we reach maturity, this concept must be taught early. On those occasions when you tell your child to do a particular chore or task and they don't do it and you get frustrated and just go on and do it yourself instead of making them do it what are you teaching? Are you teaching them an ethical approach to work? What about when your child does a slipshod job on a task and you get upset and just re-do it yourself? What are you teaching? Are you teaching an ethical approach to work? What about those times when a child might break certain rules at school and then to help the child avoid the consequences of his or her behavior, you intervene and ask school officials to let the kid have a break? Are you teaching an ethical approach to work?

You would be amazed at how many principals have told me that often kids will be late to school and even though there is a formal, written policy detailing consequences for tardiness, parents will call in or come by to ask that their kids not have to face those consequences. Often the parents will say that it was their fault the child was late because they drop their child off in the morning. It may be your fault, but late is still late. When your child grows up if they continually come to work late, ultimately the company will not be real concerned about the fact that they are late because their spouse didn't wake them up or because the dog took too long to do his business. What you teach when you intercede to help your child avoid consequences is that the rules don't apply to them. You're teaching them that if they can just point the finger in another direction and not accept responsibility for their actions, all will be well. Now, you tell me: Is that an ethical approach to work?

Here's a hint, mom and dad: If your child doesn't have to do any work around your house, it will be very difficult to later in life have an ethical approach to work.

FINANCIAL SAVVY
INTELLECTUAL CAPITAL
REALISTIC PERSPECTIVE
ETHICAL APPROACH TO WORK
D

U
P
!

Recently a human resource manager of a medium sized company mentioned to me that his company participated in a work release program with the local corrections facility. The workers they got were allowed to leave the prison grounds to come to work for the day. They then returned to lock-up for the night. He said that overwhelmingly, while on the program, the men they got were great employees. They were on time, worked hard, never took days off, had good attitudes and got along well with the other employees. As a result once they were released from jail, the company offered every one of them a fulltime, permanent position. The crazy thing though was that with the exception of one lone ranger, every one of them once they were released from lock-up became a lousy employee. Attendance and punctuality problems, attitude issues, etc.

I think we can definitely glean a lesson from this example. When they were under the control of the corrections officials, they were successful. When left to their own devices, they were miserable failures. In my mind what the corrections people represented in their lives was a DISCIPLINED LIFESTYLE. It was very clear to them, if you don't play by the rules, you are off the program and instead of leaving the jail everyday, you stay in. So they knew they had to be good employees. The correctional facility helped them have structure and order in their lives.

Interestingly, with these men the issue was not whether they could successfully and effectively do the jobs. They had already proven that. But when they were left to police themselves, it all fell apart. There was no personal discipline. What about your kids? Do they honestly have the ability to discipline themselves?

This gives us parents another challenge. We must teach our kids self-discipline. A lot of that is about establishing—and enforcing—boundaries and routine in our kids' lives. Initially when they are young we must establish and police the boundaries, but as they get older we should let them participate in setting the boundaries and allow them to police themselves. We must still be observant and when they don't police themselves properly, we must step in. It is our job as parents to get their attention. I give my girls opportunities to police themselves, but I oversee the process. Recently, I gave my youngest a task to accomplish. She dilly dallied around watching the Disney Channel and didn't do it. She then went to bed. I promptly woke her up from her wonderful sleep and made her complete her assignment. Could it have waited until the morning? Yes! But I was not trying to make things convenient for her schedule. I was teaching a lesson.

Self-discipline has always been an important trait for long-term success, but it is even more essential in today's technological environment. Most of our young people will at some point in their careers have the opportunity to work from home. They must have the focus to get up and handle their business despite all of the distractions around the house.

FINANCIAL SAVVY
INTELLECTUAL CAPITAL
REALISTIC PERSPECTIVE
ETHICAL APPROACH TO WORK
DISCIPLINED LIFESTYLE

U
P
!

The final piece of the puzzle that our kids must put together is UNDERSTANDING AND RESPECTING PEOPLE. Not just the people they like. Or the people who are just like them. Regardless of how much talent, intelligence or skills a person may have the reality of life is that there is not an awful lot they can accomplish by themselves.

Human beings were designed to be interdependent. In the workplace that interdependence is even more evident. Work, like parenting, is not a popularity contest. I have heard young people say that they quit a job—without having a new one—because they didn't like someone. So where did they get the impression that you and I liked everybody we worked with? They should work toward being likeable though. Why? Because the reality of this society we live in is that people do things for and help those people who they like. They may not like them as in bosom buddies, but they should strive to get along with all kinds of people.

I often ask managers if they had to choose between two candidates for a job and one of them was clearly better at the job, but had a poor attitude and the other was okay at the job but had a great attitude which would they select. Every manager I have ever asked that question has said they'd take the one with the good attitude. In fact, they all felt they could teach the guy with the good attitude to do the job better, but you can't teach attitude.

Everyday our world is becoming more and more diverse. It is simply reality. You don't have to like it. It is reality. Years ago in the United States diversity basically meant white and black people. Today we are diverse in so many ways that it would be in the best interest of your kids' futures and the country's future if part of your child's intellectual capital included a second or even third language, basic knowledge of the three major religions and a mind open enough to interact with anyone.

Often people say, "it's not what you know, it's who you know." Don't fool yourself, it is what you know and what you are capable of bringing to the table, but it is also who you know and who knows you and how. Relationships are critical in the workplace and in life overall. Unfortunately, a lot of our kids are picking up habits that will make it very difficult for them to develop mutually advantageous relationships. I am amazed as I travel around the country at how so many young African-American males tend to almost never smile. In fact some of them seem to keep a perpetually angry, tough, unconcerned look on their faces. Add to that how so many young men of all races are enthralled with the oversized, baggy, boxer short underneath look that is associated with the hip-hop generation. Now, get that mental image locked in and then ask yourself, how will that look impact a young man's ability to get a job?

FINANCIAL SAVVY
INTELLECTUAL CAPITAL
REALISTIC PERSPECTIVE
ETHICAL APPROACH TO WORK
DISCIPLINED LIFESTYLE
&
UNDERSTANDING AND RESPECTING
PEOPLE
!

My goal as a parent is to help my kids get to a point in their development where they are wanted. Now I know that a lot of things I've covered might make you think the future for our kids is pretty bleak. For many Americans the workplace is going to be very different and to be honest, scary. The good news is that it doesn't have to happen to your kid or mine. The problem is preventable. Completely preventable. I am convinced that if we as parents are smart for our kids when they aren't able to be they can make it in our new world. Does that sound strange to you? It shouldn't. What do you think we are doing when we childproof our homes when our babies are born? Are we not being smart for them then?

141

Remember, being smart for your kids does not mean covering for them and shielding them from facing the consequences of their behavior. Being smart for your kids means making sure they leave your nest with everything they need to be successful in this brave new world. The skills, knowledge, attitude, perspective and work ethic to be wanted. I want my kids to be FIRED UP! for their futures. So, I must continue to do my part.

You know what my biggest fear is? For those of you who only have boys, please, please make your kids wanted. The biggest fear that we fathers with daughters have is that we will do a good job with our daughters and get them prepared for the world and then they will fall in love with some boy who isn't ready for anything other than finding somebody's daughter to take over for his mother. UGH!!!!!!!

Clearly, we have a choice parents. Either we make sure our kids have the skills that will allow them to compete or we resign ourselves to being their never ending financial lifeline or bridge over troubled waters.

Personally, I choose to make sure my kids are prepared. Not just because I would like to retire comfortably some day, but also because I know that it is best for them psychologically to have goals and to reach those goals. Right now a lot of folks don't want our kids, but it does not have to be that way. The game is not over and the fat lady has not sung yet. Good luck to you. And to your kids.

Photo: Harry Langdon

Milton Creagh is a trainer and motivational speaker who annually addresses over 200,000 kids and parents worldwide. He hosted the national PBS series, *Parenting Works!* and the video-based training program, *Parent to Parent* as well as the Covenant Award winning docudrama, *Masquerade: Unveiling Our Deadly Dance With Drugs and Alcohol.*

Milton has coached a wide range of clients on reaching for their personal best, including NFL Super Bowl teams, the U.S. Conference of Mayors and incarcerated youth at juvenile detention centers. He is the national spokesman for the Parents' Resource Institute for Drug Education (PRIDE).

Visit www.miltoncreagh.com for information about Milton's forthcoming books, music releases, and other projects.